Cashmere
Kashir That Was

Cashmere Kashir That Was

by

S. Sapru

Decent Books
New Delhi

Cataloging in Publication Data — DK
[Courtesy: D.K. Agencies (P) Ltd. <docinfo@dkagencies.com>]

Sapru, S. (Somanath), 1940 -
Cashmere : Kashir that was / by S. Sapru.
xiv, 150 p. 22 cm.
Includes bibliographical references (p.)
ISBN 8186921338

1. Jammu and Kashmir (India) — History.
2. Kashmiri Pandits — India — Jammu and Kashmir — History. I. Title.

DDC 954.6 22

ISBN 81-86921-33-8
First Published in India in 2006

Published and printed by:
Decent Books
D-36/A-1, Mohan Garden
Najafgarh Road
New Delhi - 110 059
Ph. (011) 2535-3435

Distributed by:
D.K. Printworld (P) Ltd.
Regd. office : *'Sri Kunj,'* F-52, Bali Nagar
New Delhi - 110 015
Phones : (011) 2545-3975, 2546-6019; *Fax* : (011) 2546-5926
E-mail : dkprintworld@vsnl.net
Web : www.dkprintworld.com

Foreword

HAVING scrupulously gone through every line of S.Sapru's richly detailed work "Cashmere: Kashir that was," I find myself alternately laughing and (almost) crying. Laughing at all the ancient customs and manners of the true-blue Pandit and crying to realize what has happened to him since 1989-90.

What happened in the last dozen years, is nothing more and nothing less than ethnic cleansing, genocide, and trauma, but does anyone care? Has anyone ever ask the Kashmiri Pandit families what they feel? And how they are faring? No human Rights Commission seems interested in their welfare. The focus today is on Gujarat.

It is just for that reason that I am especially interested in the fate of Kashmiri Pandits. It is because reading Sapru's book has revived memories of my own people, the Goud Saraswat Brahmins.

Legend has it that my ancestors came from Kashmir, settled for a time by the river Saraswati and then moved downwards as the river began to dry up. To this day in our prayers we say :

Namostute Sharadha Devi Kashmira Puravasini

Large groups moved down towards Kutch, then to Saurashtra and Dwarka and then down to Goa where, finally, they happily settled, bringing with them their Gods.

Then came the Portuguese, and tyranny began to show itself. There were forcible conversions, acquisition of land and property and deliberate attempts by the Portuguese and

Spanish Jesuits to destroy our culture. Inquisition was the order of the day. Unable, finally, to withstand state terror, my ancestors left Goa circa 1760. Mercifully they were permitted, I understand to take with them, some of their household goods, and their Gods. They hired sea-going boats, sailed down south and in due course made their news homes in Kanara and Kerala. And many of them prospered. But they never forgot the gods they left behind. Every family had its family god and there was the *kula devata*; the *kula devata* was left behind and to this day I go to pay my obeisance to Nagesh-Mahalaxmi.

I mention all this because when I think of the Kashmiri Pandit diaspora, my mind reverts to the past and what happened to my ancestors. True, they settled down in new surroundings, accepted the new social environment, but never forgot their language — Konkani nor their culture.

The word "culture" has strong connotations. It is a way of life. And the Gaud Saraswat Brahmins had their own way of life. Young males wore their tuft — "shendi" — and became Brahmins. It must have been some time in the early twenties of the last century that it went out of fashion. When my eldest brother — some ten years senior to me — had his shendi cut off because he was being ragged by his classmates at school, my grandmother went on a fast for three days.

The purpose in recounting these facts is to draw a parallel between what the Kashmiri Pandit underwent with what Brahmins elsewhere went through, in adjusting themselves to modernity. Sapru writes: "Flexibility and adjustability has been a hallmark of the voyage of the Kashmiri Pandit through turbulent times, war, pestilence and religious persecution." At the same time, he reminds us that "orthodoxy has been the bane of the Pandit community from times immemorial." The two statements may sound contradictory but not necessarily so. They reflect two phases in the growth and development of the community.

And now reflecting of the times is the author when he says that "the pinnacle of ambition (of the Kashmiri Pandits) was to join the I.C.S"! But here it must be mentioned that what seems so typical of the Kashmiri Pandit is true also of almost all communities in India. In the twenties and thirties a member of the Indian Civil service was, in the first quarter of the twentieth century, the ambition of practically every bright young educated Indian. The appendage of the three initials I.C.S to one's name signified the ultimate in power.

To read Sapru's work is to be transported back into history, especially the history of Kashmir. it is enlightening to know that in the Kashmiri languages Kashmir is Kashir. The word was once spelt as "**Cashmere**"; Sapru deals with the origin of the more familiar word. One associated Cashmere with those exquisite shawls that cost a fortune. But it is hard to accept the belief that Kashmiris are the lost tribe of Israel. Or are they? Do they look Jewish?

What is so endearing about this book is the enormous effort that Sapru has undertaken to bring together various facets of the lives of Kashmiri Pandits. It would make any sociologist's mouth water. But the point might be made that they are not well-knit and are not inter-connected. That would be a valid complaint. And yet it is difficult to put down this book once one starts reading it for the simple reason that a surprise awaits the reader on every page.

The work may sound disjointed but that has its own special charm. Sapru is never boring. Non-Kashmiris may find all the references to customs and manners overwhelming, but one can imagine the proper Kashmiri Pandit lapping up every word, with sheer delight. Sapru has introduced to us a community and a culture in all their nuances for which we must remain ever grateful.

August 2005.

M.V. Kamath

Contents

"EXODUS, HOW MANY TIMES"

Kasheer — the glorious Kasheer
Home of Kashyap's progeny for centuries
Of all places home is the best.
Pandits nourished it with zeal and zest
By their amazing contributions
In the fields of sculpture, architecture
Philosophy, fine arts, literature
Religion, astronomy, healthcare
Pandits left a deep impress
On Kashmir's composite culture.
By dint of their hard labour
They helped Kashmir to prosper.
Once before this, once before
Zainulabedin, Budshah
Moved by justice and equity
Softened by pleadings of Sri Butt
Called Pandits back
To the forsaken Valley
Wherefrom, because of persecution
Almost the entire community
To preserve their way of life
Their age-old traditions
And the honour of their women
Had fled in different directions.

Mohan Kishan Tickoo

Acknowledgements

RIGHT from 1947, whoever left the Kashmir Valley either for studies or for a job, knew consciously that his future, now in independent India, lay beyond the Banihall Pass. It was a worrying thought, but nothing that could not be cured temporarily. Going home as a student during vacations brought back nostalgia to reality and made him feel that he had never left the Valley.

As for the man who was working anywhere else outside Kashmir, the annual leave was skillfully arranged to coincide with the summer — an occasion to meet others who were in different parts of country. It was as if we led a dual existence.

Kashmir is Home, Elsewhere is Job.

But terrorism struck its savage callous blow in 1989-90. People were dazed. Immediate physical security was a priority. After all, the noise and hubbub died out over killings, murders, rapes and destruction of property, Pandits began to wonder whether they would ever be able to reclaim their homeland.

Their Claim is Valid, but India is Deaf.

Today (2005), nearly 16 years have passed since the carnage that took place on the arrival of Pakistani terrorists and these years have been a period of reflection, regret and sadness. The numbers are slowly and steadily decreasing of those who when they meet each other ask:

Where do you live in Kashmir? The answer is "next to Darbari Kocha or opposite to Shyam Bhat's house or near Bal

Kak Dhar's house or in the lane next to Ganju House." That should tell you how Kashmiri Pandits from the Valley still identify themselves. True, this generation above 50 and 60 will soon pass on, but who will tell the children after two generations, what Sheetal Nath or Ganpatyar or the hustle and bustle of Haba Kadal or the wonderful confusion of a Batta Khandar (Pandit Wedding) was. Mental pictures of these will remain with us as long as there is life in us, but what of later?

It is with this objective in mind that I embarked on this project of leaving a record of my impressions of how Pandits lived within the seven bridges of Kashir. As most of the readers would know, there is hardly any book available on the community except for one booklet by the Wali Brothers, one book by Pandit Anand Kaul and another by Justice Jia Lal Kilam. There are thousands of books written on Kashmir, but those discuss only politics and totally ignore Pandits.

The following narrative is neither history nor a fable. It is not fiction either.

It is reality, as seen through the eyes of a growing child. The writing of this book has entailed taking help from most unlikely sources. Apart from books and newspapers, I have taken recourse to first person accounts by those whom I could persuade to put pen to paper, or talk to me.

While the thought of writing a book was there in my mind, the catalyst was a gentleman Mr. N.N. Moza who actually pushed me over the brink, and once there, there was no way but to proceed further. I tried to get help from many and wrote nearly 100 letters but only a few people kept alive my faith in the community. Apart from Mr. Moza, Dr. O.N. Wakhlu, Dr. B.N. Sharga, and D.N. Kaul answered my very basic questions about people and places in Srinagar. To veteran journalist J.N. Sadhu based at Shimla, I thank him for information on the community's outstanding teachers.

Mr. Moza and Dr. Wakhlu refreshed my childhood memories of Srinagar and its localities. Dr. Sharga gave me a great deal of information about Kashmiris, in north India. Books from the past such as Pandit Anand Kaul's book "*The Kashmiri Pandit*" and Justice Jia Lal Kilam's "*History of the Kashmiri Pandits*" provided the background of many little known details and incidents directly linked to the Pandit community.

For published sources, I would like to thank *Koshur Samachar*, New Delhi, to which I am a subscriber since many years. The journal is superb, it is a voice of the community, it is a forum for us to inform educate and entertain and maintain the vital link between ourselves. I have quoted extensively from the journal and would like to record here my thanks once again.

Vitasta of Kolkata was a mine of information, especially when I was searching for details about a great leader and social reformer of our community Kashyap Bandhu. *Vitasta* Annual Numbers are priceless sources of information, which our Biradari Association at Calcutta has so painstakingly collected, my grateful thanks to them. From Allahabad, the *Chinarika* is the organ that provided me the material I was searching for which was so generously sent to me by Col. R.K. Kak.

I would like to emphasize that any mistakes with regard to facts and interpretation in this book are mine and I accept responsibility for the same.

My special thanks go to Mr. M.P. Yashwant Kumar, former Editor of *Deccan Herald* and my mentor and senior in the profession for having gone through the manuscript in detail and checking my mistakes and suggesting placement of the written matter. Thanks are inadequate but I am sure he will understand.

Finally I would like to thank Mrs. Rathna Pushparaj and Mr. K. Pushparaj, the joint architects behind highly successful computer company, "Computron", for giving me all support to have the matter for the manuscript keyed in with the help of the staff who were very patient and hardworking.

S. Sapru

1

Wail From Vale

WHEN armed terrorists enter your house at dead of night or in broad daylight, as it happened in Kashmir in 1989-90, what do you do? Who will you ask for help? Police or the Government or the neighbours? None of them comes to help you and those whom you know, advise you to leave to save your life.

The terrorists give you a deadline. Leave by this time. If you don't, we will kill you and kidnap your womenfolk and children. You look around helpless and wonder what happened. You look at the walls, the house where you have lived for generations, full of memories and yet you know you have to leave.

You are not allowed to leave with your belongings. So you decide that saving your life and that of your family and honour is more important.

You leave with nothing, except kith and kin. But you did take something with you; MEMORIES. And till today, your mind like the computer, retrieves them, in bits and pieces.

And that is what this narrative is all about.

Why Look Back

"The further you look back into the past, the farther you can look forward into the future."

The moment a child is born and his or her mother hears the first cry, it is the beginning of a long journey in which he goes on accumulating experiences that effectively become his past.

If there was no past what would we talk about? It is the past, which when mixed with the present, eventually points to the future. And in the case of Kashmiri Pandits, an endangered species, they are in danger of losing their past after they have lost their moorings in the Kashmir Valley.

Many might question the motives for writing this book. The past cumulatively put, becomes an inheritance, a heritage that the younger generation should inherit and cherish. And it is that which gives a community a distinct identity and a link with its past.

Pandits have more than five thousand years of recorded history. They were the original inhabitants who lived in the Valley. Their way of life was distinct and as their numbers dwindled due to Muslim invasions, killing, persecution, conversion and the unsettled nature of succeeding kingdoms, provoked a fierce onslaught on their life, culture, religion, safety and freedom of the community.

There is hardly an instance where a people have been consistently targeted for religious persecution by a succession of Muslim rulers spanning nearly 600 years. From the fourteenth century to nineteenth century, barring the reign of Badshah "Zain-ul-Abidin" which provided a respite of over 50 years, all the rest were bent on wiping out the community, so much so that only 11 Pandit families were left to carry on the line at one time during the Afghan rule.

Our story here is not about history, but ourselves. Thereby of course, hangs a tale. During the first persecution in the fourteenth to fifteenth century the choice was simple.

Either convert to Islam or die. The only other choice available was to physically run away. Which is what the first wave of migrants and exiles did.

During Badshah's reign, peace prevailed and a few Pandits returned to the Valley. That brought about the division which we of this generation also know about, that is to say, Malamasies (those who stayed back despite persecution) and Bhanamis (those who left and later returned). It has been rightly said that the smaller the community, the greater the divisions.

Just after 50 years of peace during the reign of Badshah, the persecution returned with a vengeance from Aurangzeb's time and thereafter it worsened during the Afghan rule of nearly 70 years between the seventeenth and eighteenth centuries. That triggered off the second wave of migration from the Valley. In the entire history of Kashmir, from fourteenth century to nineteenth century, a relentless campaign of persecution continued against the original inhabitants with only 60 years of peace in between. It was only after the coming of Dogra rule from 1846 to 1947, a period of 101 years, that a state of peace and tranquility prevailed, during which Jammu & Kashmir emerged into the modern age. It was the catalyst called Biscoe who strode like a colossus and pitchforked Kashmir into the twentieth century.

The third wave of migration came in 1947 at the time of the Kabailie invasion. After that, migration was slow but peaceful over a period of 45 years. The last migration took place and degenerated into an exodus in the winter of 1989-90.

Wherever we are scattered around India and abroad in various countries, each one of us carries his heritage, culture and identity with him. Today, our surnames and our faces identify us from a distance. But each one of us knows what we have left behind in our native land, the land of rivers and mountains, the land of chinars, and Deodars, poplars and mulberry, the numerous kinds of flowers and **"the ashes of our fathers and the temples of our Gods."**

When you lose something, which is material, which you can see, which you can taste, and which has through generations become a part of you, *all that you can take with you are the memories.* Can't we at least have them, savour them, and recall them with nostalgia. We can be allowed to do that because these memories are now a part of our heritage.

The Pandit community can proudly boast of writers, historians, poets and generally men of letters, intellectuals and journalists but sadly we have only three history books written by Pandits about their own community, although many books on Kashmir, its politics, its geography and its general history have been written by Kashmiri Pandit authors. The first is Wali, I.K., and Wali, M.K.: "Kashmiri Pandits — A Social Survey," Lahore, 1917. This was perhaps the first written record of the community specifically. After this, came Pandit Anand Kaul who wrote the book "The Kashmiri Pandit" in 1924 which was followed by another book entitled "History of Kashmiri Pandits" by Justice Jia Lal Kilam in 1955. All three were results of individual and private enterprise.

In the post independence period, several books on Kashmiri Pandits have been written, but I have only consulted Dr. Kusum Pant's doctoral thesis in Australia. However whatever I have quoted from her, concerns the early exiles from the sixteenth, seventeenth and eighteenth centuries who settled down in various parts of north India and did their utmost to uplift themselves economically and still retain their identity.

What will happen on the ground in the future, we do not know, but at least we do have especially for those children who will be born in the future, something to tell them who their people were. A key to the past, a glimpse of the old panorama, and a window through which to recognize our identity.

And so, here we are, looking at **Cashmere** of yore, (Kashir, that is) and a narrative about the life and times of Kashmiri Pandits through the eyes of one who saw it all and through others who experienced it from time to time, natives and visitors, rulers and the ruled. In short, a community which was at home and is now in exile.

2

Kashyap Rishi's Bhoomi

THE beautiful Valley of Kashmir, which is today witnessing blood-curdling events, caught the imagination of writers and poets as early as the eleventh century, if not earlier. Kalhana, who wrote the history of Kashmir in verse a round about the year 1149, has this to say:

> Such is Kashmir, the country which may be conquered by the force of spiritual merit but not by armed force. . . . where there are not baths in winter: comfortable landing places on the river banks, where the rivers being free from aquatic animals are without peril; where realizing that the land created by his father is unable to bear heat the hot-rayed sun honours it by bearing himself with softness even in summer. Learning, high dwelling-houses, saffron, iced water, grapes and the like — what is commonplace there, is difficult to secure in paradise. . . .

Kashmir is a paradise on earth, this is how Kashmir has been described by renowned writers, both Indian and those from outside. One version has it that the name Kashmir is derived from Sanskrit meaning water and shimira meaning to drain. Geologists have confirmed that the valley was once a lake and when it dried up it became habitable. It is said that Buddhism came to Kashmir in the wake of Ashoka's conquest in 250 BC and it is well known that Ladakh is still Buddhist by faith.

The Jammu and Kashmir state, to give it its full name, is the northern most part of India and has an area of 84, 471 sq.

miles. Much of the sufferings of its people are due to its extremely strategic location. The Kashmir valley is surrounded by hilly and mountainous terrain. The areas of Jammu, Poonch, Muzaffarabad, Gilgit, Baltistan and Ladakh constitute the ring of highlands that stand sentinel over the Valley and border on Pakistan, Afghanistan and the Sinkiang and Tibet parts of China. Only a few miles separate it from the territory of the USSR, the Central Asian Republics of Tajikistan, Turkmenistan and Uzbekistan being the nearest.

Why Kashmiri Pandits & not Kashmiri Brahmins

Actually, the appellation is a little over 200 years old. As per historical records, the decadent Mughal emperor, Mohammad Shah (1719-48), applied it for the first time and that too at the behest of one of his most trusted and favourite courtiers, Shri Jai Ram Bhan, who at that time was considered to be the main representative of all those Kashmiri Pandits who had left the Valley to seek the patronage of the Mughal kings and got settled in Delhi and in some other adjoining cities permanently along with their families.

> By their administrative capabilities and command over the Persian language, these Pandits inveigled themselves into the good grace and favours of the Mughals and thereby considered themselves to be superior to other Brahmins. To maintain their superior position in society and to establish their higher claims and status to dominate other caste groups, Shri Bhan prevailed upon Mohammad Shah to issue a "Shahi Ferman" (royal decree) identifying them as Kashmiri Pandits. This was just to maintain their distinct ethnic individuality from the other categories of Brahmins. After all, a superior breed is recognized all over the world.
>
> — Dr. B.N. Sharga, *Koshur Samachar*, Feb. 2000.

Cashmere, Kashmir, Kashmeer, Kushmir or Kushmere?

The Webster English Language Dictionary defines Cashmere

as "Shawl, soft fabric of goat's hair." Only after that does it give the name and spelling as "Kashmir."

Because of the Kashmiri Shawl connection with France the soft wool was identified as Cashmere and for some time the word was spelt so in writing, newspapers, journals, books etc., as late as the early twentieth century, newspapers like The Times of India, Statesman & The Pioneer, and C & M Gazette spelt it so. However Kashmiris themselves pronounce it as Kushmir, and in Kashmiri the word is Kashir.

Jia Lal Kilam says in his book "*The Kashmiri Pandit*:"

> Pandit Raj Kak was appointed as Governor of Kamraj, but after a short time he was placed in charge of the Shawl department. He raised the income of this department from four lacs to twelve lacs.

The Kashmiri shawl was much prized in Europe. Even Queen Victoria had made a rule to present a shawl as a wedding gift to any princess of royal blood, and thus its use came into vogue in England. But its chief market was France and the French traders used to depute their agents to Kashmir directly from France. The defeat of France in AD 1870 in the Franco-Prussian war spelt ruin to the industry in Kashmir.

> The deputation of the French agents to Kashmir brought the Kashmiri Pandits face to face with European culture and literature. Hitherto their literary pursuits were limited to knowledge of Persian and Sanskrit, but now with fresh opportunities they began to study French and other European languages.

One has to recall that in the nineteenth century French influence in Europe was so great, so much so that it became the language of diplomacy and communication between nations, a lingua franca, because of which Kashmir was spelt as Cashmere for which one of the catalysts was the shawl trade connection with the Valley. Hence, its use as the title of this book.

3

"Yemen Sattan Kadalan Munz"
Within These Seven Bridges

THE lifestyle for generations of Kashmiri Pandits was frugal and in close harmony with nature. Kashmir is perhaps the only place where houses were designed to meet the changes in weather by using locally available material. Most traditional houses had thatched roofs. There was no cement concrete. The first layer of the roof was covered with birch bark, which provided not only cover, but also insulation during winter. Over this layer, was a thick coating of earth, which was pasted together with mud, that after drying would hold together and over a period of time one could see even grass and plants growing on the roof. During winter and the rainy season, surplus water would drain off and even a snowfall would not be able to penetrate the roof.

The design of the house was such that no matter how poor the owner and how small the house, it had to have three separate distinct divisions. The ground floor usually had on the right side the living room where the family gathered to eat, children played and neighbours and visitors would drop in for a chat. This was called "wot." Adjacent to it was the kitchen. The first floor of the house contained the bedrooms for sleeping. The second floor of the house was an exact replica of the ground floor with a living room and a kitchen. This was called "kaeni." Due to severe winters, the ground floor was used during the cold season. As soon as summer came, the family would shift to the second floor. This was an ideal arrangement. Unfortunately, cement concrete has totally pushed this practical and useful arrangement out.

Between 1877 and 1927 is a time span of half a century. In 1877, there were no cars and no telephones. All transportation was done by tongas, carriages and carts. The Valley was cut off for more than six months in a year due to snow from the Jammu side, but fortunately, the Muzaffarabad, Domel road across the Kohala Bridge on the Jhelum Valley Road used to remain open during winter to facilitated supplies of essential articles. The tunnel on top of the Pir Panjal was built in 1892. . . .

In 1892, Maharaja Pratap Singh asked for a British engineer to help link up the two sides of the Pir Panjal. What he built was not a tunnel in the real sense of the word, but an arch with open spaces in its spans that gave a partial cover and kept the road open during mild snowfall. Although this was called the Banihall Tunnel, it was not a regular tunnel. It was only in 1953, that the Government of India called in a German-Swiss company M/s. Karl Kunz, to survey the mountain and build the tunnel.

The original arch was built at a height of over 9,000 ft. and the German engineers bored a tunnel at a height of 7,000 ft., which eventually saved about 30 miles in travel over perilous hairpin bends. This tunnel was after completion inaugurated in 1956 with a two-way road for incoming and outgoing traffic.

Life in the early part of the century was a curious mixture of the desire to remain secure, and contented within limited means. As can be seen from census records, Pandits numbered roughly about 50,000 in the entire valley in 1901, this went up to over 54,000 in 1921, a span of one generation. The curious thing about the 1921 census was that more Pandits were living in the rural areas than in Srinagar. This trend changed within a span of 30 years with more and more people, especially the young ones who had gone to school and college, migrating to Srinagar in search of employment.

There was very little contact with the outside world. When Dr. Gasha Lal and Dr. S.N. Peshin, went to England for higher studies in medicine it created a stir within the community. But when R.C. Kak, who later became the second Kashmiri Pandit (he was from the Valley) to become the Prime Minister of Jammu and Kashmir in the twentieth century, and L.N. Zutshi married an English woman, the community was scandalized, but since both of them were affluent nothing much came out of it. The reason is very simple. The Pandit is always conscious of rank and both of these gentlemen had the rank.

In 1877, and right through to the end of the nineteenth century and the beginning of the twentieth century till 1947, the turban was the normal headgear for every Kashmiri Pandit. There are some old faded photographs of the earliest batches of students who passed out of the Mission School at Fateh Kadal showing all Pandit students wearing turbans.

The dress for the male was a shirt and a pyjama with a sweater and a coat during cold weather but the majority preferred, unless they had to go to office, wearing a pheran and, if it was below zero temperature, a thick woolen blanket over it. Wearing leather was originally taboo but as time went on they were allowed, outside the house, shoes, long boots, belts, halters and whips during the glorious horse era. Of course, on reaching home, everybody had to take the shoes off at the entrance or in the passage near the door on the ground floor.

The footwear was the interesting part of the dress. Those living in the villages used a modified kind of Paizar, a native shoe with a long nose, and in summer quite a few used to wear khadaon (wooden clogs) Patan Gapal. In town, that is Srinagar, most of the old fashioned types used an open shoe without shoelaces, which was strangely enough called "Panditji Boot." Fashion, they say, goes round in circles. The same Panditji Boot has now become so popular in India that most executives prefer it. Today it is called "Slipons."

This was in the thirties and forties but in the two decades before that which ended in 1920 it was slightly different. At home, going to the bazaar and moving around in your Mohalla, it was the *Khrave* — the wooden sandal with a small strap, but one has to remember that this was a symbol of progress. What it replaced was indeed a device that had lasted amongst the people in the Kashmir Valley for almost 5000 years.

What I Am Talking About?

It was the unique ***Pulhoru*** It was made of grass. It had pleats and it had a sole, which provided the foot firm grip when walking. Especially on frozen chunks of ice. Most Pandits living in villages used it as did most in Srinagar. But the march of time changed it gradually from Pulhoru to Khrave to Leather chappal and Leather boot.

What was the daily routine like in those days? The majority of those living in Srinagar were clerks and petty officials in the State Government, the Srinagar Municipality, and after 1911 the Shali Store, the Accountant General's office. In the rural areas, those who had some land, supervised farming operations in summer and just passed the days in winter when the fields were covered with snow.

But even here the children were sent to school and very often one would find a Pandit farmer who would also be a village Primary School teacher and his children would aspire for a job in the city. That explains the seeming paradox of the 1921 census, which revealed more Pandits in Villages than in Srinagar City.

The street scene would reflect the daily routine of most city Pandits. From early morning on working days the traffic by foot would start by about 9.00 A.M. with clean-shaven Pandits wearing European clothes but wearing a turban walking briskly towards the Secretariat. The procession of these employees would draw them from Chattabal, Ali Kadal and Rainawari as also other areas such as Habba Kadal etc.

Two points remain to be explained: Right up to 1947, the headgear was an important part of a man's dress and the majority wore turbans. A few of the younger lot in the forties went in for caps. My father and my uncle both sported turbans right up to 1947. My father gave up the turban, but my uncle was more tradition bound and continued to wear the turban till the day he died.

During the 1830s, G.T. Vigne, an employee of the East India Company, came to Kashmir and his description is apt: "Independently of the forehead-mark, there is a difference in the style of the turban. The Hindu smooths it over the right temple, the Musalman on the left. There is also a distinction in wearing the tunic: the Musalmans tie it on the right side, whilst that of the Hindu's is folded over to the left breast."

The second point relates to transport. In most princely states, in the capital city, there was no organized Municipal Bus Service. Strangely enough the city of Bangalore was similarly placed because most of the employees lived within walkable distance from the Secretariat at Bangalore, which was then called Attara Kacheri. They would eat their lunch in the morning and walk to the Secretariat. There was no city bus either in Bangalore or in Srinagar.

In the Kashmir Valley, because of lack of railways, the bus services were the first to reach Srinagar and other smaller towns, but the ordinary man had still to walk and the slightly affluent ones could hire a tonga. There were no rickshaws, only horse drawn vehicles. When finally the Municipal Bus Service was inaugurated in the seventies, the initial minimum for a ticket was one Anna. The housewives looking at the novelty of the bus going through the narrow lanes of the city promptly nicknamed the bus "Ponde Bus". The word Ponde means one Anna. In effect, it was the one-Anna bus. Subsequently autos and taxis appeared although the latter was there earlier but mainly meant for tourists.

One of the greatest ambitions of the Pandit was to secure a Government job and in the small marriage market, a boy who had a Government job, no matter how low became an eligible bachelor to be sought out by anxious parents with daughters of marriageable age. There is a wrong impression that Pandits held a monopoly over jobs. True a large number of them were physically present in these jobs but most of them were at the clerical level. There was hardly any technicians leave alone any engineers or officers.

The majority of them would start as clerks and after about twenty years be promoted to head clerk, which was a great occasion for rejoicing, and finally retire in that post. A few lucky ones would retire as Office Superintendent. Today this post is called Section Officer.

The initial grade was 25-2-55. This was where the majority of Pandits began their careers in Government Service. The next grade was 40-4-80 and this was for the favoured few. The few Pandits who took up unusual professions like Police (Uniformed) and technicians at the Overseer (today this post is called Junior Engineer) level, the higher grade of 80-8-200 was applicable.

A Handful of Rice (Mochchaphol)

A drop of water is all alone, weak and ineffective. When other drops join it, it becomes stronger and when many more join it becomes an ocean. So is it with public social causes, which Kashyap Bandhu espoused. When he had no money for social work or for his paper Martand, he asked the people to contribute a handful of rice.

Kashyap Bandhu can claim credit for starting the custom and practice of Mochchaphol but in reality the programme was Shyamlal Gurtu's brain child. The meaning of Mochchaphol is fistful of rice in the Kashmiri context. Shyamlal was very eager to raise a fund for the welfare of poor families of the *Biradari*. He agreed with the saying that charity begins at home. At the same time, he was conscious that it should also begin from that home from which it is proclaimed. But he didn't have enough money to open the fund.

> He was not employed in any government or private institution that could have been a source of his income. He was dependent on the income from his agricultural land, which was in the form of farm produce rather than cash. It may be for this very reason that Shyamlal Gurtu, instead of collecting money from the affluent class of the Biradari for its needy members, launched a mass campaign for collection of handful of rice from very household every month and himself contributed one or two treks (approx. 5kgs.) of rice every time. He was very generous in sharing the yield of paddy from his field with others every autumn. In the times of scarcity of food grains in the valley, which was a common phenomenon those days, he used to help his needy neighbours and relatives with bags of rice free of cost and to not so needy persons on nominal price and that too on credit which they seldom cleared.
>
> — Harikrishna Kaul, *Koshur Samachar*, Septermber 2001.

The next grade was, 80-8-200. This was the grade that paved the way to the Gazetted Officers' rank. My own father was in a grade, which till today I have not been able to fathom. The next in line was 150-10-250, which was a dream few could attain though many might aspire for it.

My father's grade in force with the Kashmir Government was 200-20-300 and it was in operation till the late seventies. Simple arithmetic will tell you that within five years an officer will go from the minimum to the maximum of the Grade and then what happens to him. In Government Service, they happily vegetate and stagnate.

Life was hard, Life was simple, but it had its rewards. The entire cycle of twelve months was divided into two parts summer and winter. The high point of it was the magic words "Durbar Move." This was an innovation created by political compulsions of the ruling Dogra dynasty. While summer and winter are a part of the seasons, the exact six-month division came after the Kashmir Valley was added to the Dogra state of Jammu and formed the composite state of Jammu and Kashmir in 1846.

It was Maharaja Pratap Singh who introduced the Durbar move. Srinagar became the summer capital and Jammu the winter capital of the state. On November 5th, of every year the office would move to Jammu and May 5th the Office would reopen in Srinagar. Since most of the Pandits were clerks in the State Government, their life was accordingly regulated. Quite often in every family one or two brothers would be in those departments which would move to Jammu and a third brother would be employed in Srinagar itself. This would ensure that the family home was occupied and protected.

While those who went to Jammu enjoyed milder weather during winter, those who were left behind had to face the combined rigours of *chille kalan, chille khorad, chille bache* for ninety days. These were the divisions made to measure the intensity of cold in winter. The first one, *kalan,* was the most severe part of winter, which lasted forty days followed by *khorad,* which lasted thirty days and *bache,* which lasted twenty days.

Winter was a time of misery. Actually, one had to make preparations for winter in the Kashmir Valley just as one makes preparations for a North Pole or an Everest expedition. As soon as October came, the family head would start buying firewood.

This used to be one of the little excitements for children when the huge blocks of wood were brought and dumped into the yard or *aangan*. The children would watch as the lumberjacks chopped the logs with their massive axes. After that, the women of the house had to carry the bits and pieces of *zuin* (firewood) inside the house. This was a priority job and once finished, the man could heave a sigh of relief. In some houses, an underground room called *gaan* was used to store firewood.

On the food front, many more preparations had to be made. Those kinds of edibles had to be purchased and stored which would survive the severe winter. Apart from rice, the only other item that was readily available for storage was Rajma and, damma and things like *hogadde* (dried fish). Aside from this, potatoes and shalgam (vegetables) were purchased in large quantities and put in for long-term preservation.

The preservation of some of the foodstuffs was done in the most innovative manner. At the back of every house, there used to be a small piece of land covered by a projection or ledge, which generally was a small addition to the main room on the first floor. This was called a *Dub*. Here a small trench was dug. Into this trench, bags of potatoes and Shalgam were kept with a wooden plank for cover. As and when required, the housewife would go out and get her daily requirement from the trench. Which is called *Khave* in Kashmiri.

It needs to be mentioned that before 1947 nobody in the Kashmir Valley would ever touch a chapatti. We were hundred percent rice eaters. It was only in 1947 when supplies were stopped by Pakistan that people gradually started eating wheat because of shortage of rice.

One more thing. In the rest of India, when we talk of *Dal Roti* it means that *dal* is a staple part of food and takes the place of *sabzi* (vegetable) in poorer households. In the valley *dal*, was practically unknown and on rare occasions the doctor would prescribe it for a patient who was recovering from an illness. What is *dal roti* in the rest of India, is *Haak Batha*, in Kashmir. *Haak* is sag, a green vegetable which is leafy, very rich in iron and used to be cheap and easily available. This and rice was the staple diet of all the people in the valley as meat and fish though available were expensive. For most people, because the poor are always more in number, it was always a struggle between the menu and the money, literally between *haak* and *rogan josh*.

Vanguj (Tenant)

Till 1947, there was hardly any person in Kashmir valley who would rent out his home or part of his home to a tenant. Only in rare cases, especially in the Civil line areas, would outsiders be able to get accommodation on rent.

It is a measure of the distinction of Kashmir Valley that there was hardly anybody who did not possess his own shelter over his head. Everybody had a home and the idea of renting out a part of his home for money was totally repugnant and socially unacceptable. This writer had for the first time come across this word, Vanguj when the Pakistani invasion of Kashmir took place in 1947. At that time, a number of Pandit families from the rural areas like Baramulla, Bandipur or Kupwara fled to Srinagar for security.

Gone are the days when a tenant as a rare case would stick out like a sore thumb as neighbours would ask each other as to who he was. The Answer would come "yumin ha chu vanguj vore" (These people have a tenant).

Today there is a sea change. Renting houses is a source of income.

Give and Take

Whenever the marriage of a son or a daughter was to be performed in a family, all the kith and kin would attend the function and offer small sums of money to the head of the family. This was called *gulimyuth*. Although this paltry amount did not pinch the purse of the person who paid it, put together, this would amount to a substantial sum that gave financial succour to the *yajmaan* (Head of the Family) when he needed it most.

The other useful custom was the payment of wurehbal, which was yet, another contribution made by the relatives and friends towards the expenditure incurred in the running of the kitchen temporarily set up for cooking for various functions connected with the marriage. For cooking for hundreds of relatives, friends and neighbours, a chulah consisting of two parallel rows of bricks bound with clay was temporarily erected and firewood was burnt in it. Called wureh in Kashmiri, the small contribution towards expenses was thus named wurehbal. Gulimyuth and wurehbal gave much financial relief to the family who had to marry their wards. However, the amount of such contributions was limited. For instance, wurehbal was fixed at Re1 for both the rich and the poor, who were called ***safed posh*** as they wore white clothes. Gulimyuth could vary between a relative and a friend or an acquaintance.

As every family had to perform a marriage or two in its life-time, it was a matter of give and take for everyone. Each got this financial help when his turn came and none felt humiliated while accepting this amount. On the other hand, such customs were ingenious devices invented to firmly cement the bonds of kinship and close-knit Biradari. There is a saying that a friend in need is a friend indeed. To this, I would like to add that friends and relatives those days were real friends and relatives. That is why there is a saying in Kashmiri: *Zardar marih magar kachdar marih neh*. *Zardar* means a rich man and *kachdar* means one who has many kith and kin. The saying literally means that a person having abundant money can die but one having kith and kin will not.

Partners in Adversity

It was not only on happy occasions like marriage and *yagnopavit* (thread)ceremonies that the relatives and friends shared the burdens, but they were partners in adverse moments as well. When a family lost one of its members, their relatives and friends participated in the mourning not only physically but also mentally and financially. On the tenth day, kriya was performed in the nearest river as is the practice even now. All the relatives, friends and neighbours used to attend the function at the ghat. When the kriya was over, the person who performed it would walk from the river ghat towards his home and all the people assembled there followed him up to the gate. Here, they divided themselves in two parallel rows creating a narrow passage in between. The bereaved person would enter his house and come out wearing a pheran with his blanket and wearing a wooden sandal (*khrave*) on his feet. He would then walk from one end of the passage, formed by the two human walls, to the other when moving in one direction, the pocket of his pheran faced towards one row of his relatives and friends and while coming back it faced towards the other row. Each person in the two rows would put his closed fist in his pocket and drop some money in the pocket when the person passed by. Although like *gulimyuth* and *wurehbal*, the amounts were small on this occasion also, yet, because of a large network of kith and kin, especially due to joint families, such small sums of money were like little drops of water making a veritable ocean. This money helped the family in the smooth performance of the kriya on the eleventh and twelfth days, which used to be quite elaborate.

Sense of Brotherhood.

During those days, the members of our community did not possess sufficient sources of income and a majority of them needed financial assistance to perform various social and religious rituals. As such, these contributions came in handy to save the biradari from the clutches of moneylenders. Moreover, this inculcated a sense of partnership in happiness as well as in gloom, which is missing these days to a great extent. Some of us may have improved our financial position substantially, but have no peace of mind, which our ancestors had in abundance, even with limited sources of income.

The Ugly Face of Persecution

- *No Hindu should ride a horse, nor should a Hindu wear a shoe;*
- *That they should not wear Jama (an article of Mogul dress);*
- *That they should not bear arms;*
- *That they should not visit any garden;*
- *That they should not have Tilak mark on their foreheads;*
- *That their children should not receive any education.*

Muhatta Khan

He was just a usurper who overthrew the Subedar and through rabble rousing, persecuted, murdered, killed and plundered the lives and property of Kashmiri Pandits in the first half of the eighteenth century when Mughal rule over Kashmir had become shaky.

4

Of Things Native

Kangri and Pheran

Kangri is a Sanskrit word meaning a fireplace first used by Upadeva. To a Kashmiri, nothing is more indigenous and, therefore, typically Kashmiri than *Kangri*, the fire-pot. It is the result of experience spread over a very long time that made this article of creative genius possible. The *Kangri* is a combination of baked-mud and wicker. *Manan* was the ancestor of the *kangri*. The earthen pot around which *hatab* twigs are woven is called *kundal* in Kashmiri and the *Kangri* makers are known as *Kanil*. They live mostly on the banks of the Wular Lake in the villages of Watlab and Botingo where women and children help in *Kangri* making.

In Tsrar village, a special kind of *Kangri* is manufactured, which is known for its white wicker and colour shine. The stout *Kangri* is known as *Grees-i-Kangri*. It is almost double the size of an ordinary *Kangri*. It is kept under the pheran, the outer garment of a Kashmiri The *Kangri* gives warmth from the burning charcoal inside and the degree of warmth varies. More than 500 families are engaged in *Kangri* making. They use *pohu, lim, kachu* and *hatab* in the form of twigs round the earthen pot.

The *Kangri* clings to a Kashmiri as an object of perfection in indigenous art. Mysticism has shadowed the genius of Kashmir in the past and the five ribs of *Kangri* represent five elements that make the universe. The pot suffering patiently with fire is the goddess Shakti held fast by the masculine wicker frame — Shiva. It is believed that women have contributed to the perfection of this fine piece of art. — G.T. Vigne, *Travels in Kashmir, Ladak, Iskardo*.

Pheran

Thermal underwear, internal heating, electrical gadgets are all part of the modern armoury to combat cold. In Kashmir Valley, European clothing is still used (2003) during office hours, but at home the dressing gown is for show whereas the sweet pheran is for warmth.

What is a pheran? A long loose fitting garment with wide arms and open collar. It can be worn by bending and pulling it over your head. There are two types of pheran, one for the winter which is made of wool with a cotton lining inside (called poch), the second one made to the same specification but made of cotton. Form the head it goes down and reaches just below your knees.

Since both men and women wear the pheran, it is necessary to differentiate between the male and the female apparel. While the male *pheran* is plain, and comes down to the knee, the female one is longer and decorated around collar with broad sleeves. It is called in Kashmiri *Naware*.

The happiest combination is the pheran and the *Kangri*, which under the cover of pheran provides the heat.

Let the Chille Kalan come, my pheran and my kangri will fight it.

Ai kangri! Ai kangri!	"O, kangri! O, kangri!"
Kurban tu Houris wu Peri!	You are the gift of Houris and Fairies
Chun dur bughul mi girim	When I take you under my arm,
Durd az dil mi buree.	You drive fear from my heart.

— *Geography of Jammu and Kashmir*, by A.N. Raina.

Tea Tales

The cup that cheers but does not inebriate is the ideal nightcap in the Kashmir Valley when the air has a nip in the evenings. Flavoured with cinnamon, cardamom and almonds (crushed), the Kashmiri *chai* has a flavour, all its own.

The *pahari chai*, as it is popularly called, is boiled in the *samavar*, which with its aquiline nose and hourglass figure has today become an item of decoration in the plains. Not so in Kashmir, where the needed charcoal is available. Milk is, however, used by Kashmiris in preparing what is called sheer *chai*. It attains a pinkish colour, thanks to the use of bicarbonate of soda. Salt is added to taste. In the tele-serial, *Gul Gulshan Gulfam*, a boatwoman was seen serving this tea.

It is the sugared "*chai*" sans milk, also called *Kahwa* which has its confirmed, traditional devotees abroad. Travelling through Turkey, in the early 70s, we found chai restaurants quite popular in the countryside. Thanks to our Urdu base, we spoke Turkish without an accent — a fact appreciated by the Turks, who are as proud of their language as are the French. Chai is served in cups called fincan ('c' pronounced as 'j'), placed in saucers containing sugar cubes and spliced lemon, to be consumed to taste.

Just as the Turks use the word *chai* so do Russians. In Moscow, we came across sugared chai served in glasses, neatly balanced in decorated containers. Since they too use the word chai, it was easy to ask for it. A huge samovar was in use in the restaurant, flames leaping from the burning charcoal inside it. I also came to know that Russians use the word "*kulich*" for sweet cake as do the Kashmiris, the only difference being that theirs is soft and more sugared. Mentally traversing to the British *cuppa*, part and parcel of the British way of life, one ponders over the social etiquette that goes with the tea ceremony. Even the milk pot has to have a cosy! I am reminded of one Shri Ram, Scout Commissioner of J&K in the late 30s and early 40s, who had been directly appointed by Maharaja

Hari Singh. His dominant passion, rather, mission, was to wean Kashmiris from the chai drinking habit. He lived in a houseboat-cum-hotel, moored near Amira Kadal, then the first bridge of Srinagar. He would demonstrate to us boy scouts, how to make tea by boiling dried pieces of skin of oranges or rind of apples. He was avuncular, affectionate, wearing a small turban and a close-cut moustache. Shri Ram was a popular figure in the Valley also in Jammu and Ladakh - but he never realized that his was a mission foredoomed to failure. — Somnath Dhar, 19.12.92, *Indian Express*.

Hubble Bubble

The British rule in India produced in the English language many new words which originated from Indian language words and got absorbed in the English language.

One of these deserves a mention because it also acts as a link with Kashmir. Try this for size. Water pipe. Now we know that the British colonial culture had the cigar and the pipe as part of the living routine. After dinner, cigar or pipe with brandy was a part of the living culture. Tobacco as such has been part of mankind and it was only in the twenties of the twentieth century that the cigar got miniaturized to cigarette, and became very popular worldwide. It also came to Kashmir. While the younger ones started smoking cigarettes, the older ones also continued to consume tobacco but in the traditional way.

And that brings us to the hubble bubble. The Colonial Sahib had already seen this device or contraption in countries like Turkey, Egypt and Afghanistan and also in the rest of India. With his stiff upper lip, the sahib called it the water pipe, but the natives who knew a bit of English noted the sounds emanating from the contraption and rightly named it hubble bubble.

Of course, the traditional name for it in north India is *hookah* but let us find out what this *hookah* is and how it operates.

A round metal pot is filled with water and it is corked at the top with a pipe leading from it to end with a holder on which is generally perched a small round earthen pot in which tobacco in a slightly wet state is put, over which glowing coals are put that starts processing the tobacco. At the bottom of the round pot, another pipe comes out with a nozzle at the end, which a person puts in his mouth and draws as one would draw, smoke from cigarette. This process produces a sound similar to the words hubble bubble. And hence the name. The proper name is *Tamaek Jajir*. The perch at the top in which tobacco is put is called a chillum which today adorns the Oxford English dictionary.

Even today (2005) there are many faithful adherents to the hookah as there are to the hubble bubble in the Kashmir Valley. In the rest of India too, it is very much there. If you do not belive me, take a good look at Shriman Mahender Singh Tikait, the famous farm leader from U.P sitting on his charpoy and dispending political wisdom in the company of his Hookha.

Samavar*

The samavar of Kashmir is certainly an eighteenth century importation from Russian lands via Central Asia. But it appears that Kashmiri metal workers made some changes in its size and form. The type of samavar we have today is not to be found in Central Asia. But certainly the cup called *pyaleh* in Central Asia and in Kashmir is identical in shape and size. In Kashmir, it is called *Chinpyaleh* thereby indicating its Chinese origin. The fact of the matter is that it must have been brought for the first time from Yarkand or Kashghar, which lie in Eastern Turkestan, with which regions we had a brisk trade in medieval times and which in turn were very close to Chinese mainland. They might have brought it from China, named it Chinpyaleh and passed it on to Kashmir. Pandits have the

* The word samavar is the way it is spoken in Kashmiri. In Russian and English, it is spelt as samovar.

Khos instead of Pyaleh but then Khos is the corrupted form of Persian kaseh pronounced as khaseh — *Vitasta*, Dr. K.N. Pandit 1999-2000.

Dhoonga (House boat)

Noah's ark may have been the first boat in history or legend according to Western sources, but in Indian history and folklore, boats were present in the times of *Ramayana* and *Mahabharata*.

In the Kashmir Valley with its many rivers, lakes and waterways, boats have been around for a long time. A normal ordinary boat to carry people or light loads are called *shikara*s. *Shikara*s are narrow at both ends and wide in the middle for balancing the weight.

The *dhoonga* is the bigger version built on the same lines, but with greatly increased capacity for people not only to live, but also to carry passengers and loads. In Kashmir, a small community called Hanjis, who are professionally and traditionally boatmen, also live in dhoongas. Often even today, you can see dhoongas tied up on the Jhelum river or the various canals where people sit, sleep, cook and make it their floating home.

Until the advent of the British, the *dhoonga* ruled the roost. However, when Tyndale Biscoe arrived, he introduced British designs for rowing boats and bigger cutters. His pioneering work **(sadly not remembered or acknowledged by the Kashmir Government even today)** encouraged the modern houseboat design to come to Kashmir. The basic difference between the *dhoonga* and the houseboat is that, the latter has more flat space inside to accommodate European furniture like chairs, tables, and beds as also toilet and bathing facilities.

Houseboats are for tourists. *Dhoonga*s are for natives. Though the houseboat has now been around for nearly 80 years, it has not been able to make a dent into the seniority and position of the native boat. **Long live the *dhoonga*.**

5

The Way We Were

Orthodoxy versus Modernism

TODAY, most middle class Indians wear European clothing during working hours and traditional dresses at home. Over a period of time, it was discovered that European clothing was economical and smart, it also made a man feel active. During the 90 years of British rule, most English educated Indians blindly aped the Englishmen even to the extent of wearing a dressing gown, when it was sweltering hot.

After Independence, gradually European clothing was adjusted to the needs of weather and climate. It was unthinkable in those days to see a man going to office wearing open sandals but today the entire accent is on practicality and utility. If one looks carefully around, one will see that there is a resurgence of pride in Indian clothing and on appropriate occasions Indians take pride in wearing Kurtha Churidhar and other traditional forms of dress such as the Waistcoat (Jawahar Jacket) made popular during the forties by Jawaharlal Nehru. Added to that is now the close collar coat.

Flexibility and adjustability has been a hallmark of the passage of the Kashmiri Pandit through turbulent times, peaceful times, war, pestilence and religious persecution. During the Mughal rule, the dress code conformed to that of the conquerors. Subsequently, this form continued with the headgear (turban) worn in different ways. While the Purana Kashur who had migrated to the plains during Aurangzeb's rule had already started their march towards English education in the late nineteenth century, the Tazu Kashur lagged behind by about two generations. English education on a fairly noticeable scale began to make an impact from about 1910.

Thus it was that among most of the office going clerks, assistants and others such as teachers who wore pant and the coat, the only acknowledgement to tradition was the continuation of the turban. By and large most Kashmiri Pandits were in the clerical scale and hence could not be called gazetted officers. One of the unwritten codes seems to have been that one wore a necktie if one was a gazetted officer.

Some of the other items of European apparel made their appearance in isolation and those who used them were at first gaped at. But once it caught on, it was imitated. The case of the night suit and the dressing gown is interesting. For a while during weddings, the son in law was presented night suits and some families did start using it. But today it has come in full circle and most people wear kurtha and Pyjama.

What was the impact of such practices on the small Kashmiri Pandit community in the valley?. It is best that we hear about the reaction to foreign ideas and practices from Pandit I.K. Wali and M.K. Wali who were perhaps the first in the community to write a brochure entitled *"The Social Survey of the Kashmiri Pandits"*

A father asked his son, who had just returned from England, to wash and come to the *chauki* (a piece of wood on hinges suitable for eating on the floor) to have his food and can you imagine what his reply was? "No, thank you, father," he said, "I can as easily sit at the dining table." The father was, no doubt, stunned with the reply, but this was not the only reply; another came to him later. "Come here, my son, put on your *dhoti* and go to bed," said the fond parent. "Excuse me, my father, I have got my night-suit with me," was the reply.

Once, the same father was taking a walk along the bazaar when a clean-shaven Kashmiri youth, whom he knew to be a fast friend of his son, and as one who was distinguished in his educational career by having been thrice plucked in the matriculation Examination, cut him on the way. His accomplishments seemed to bear a marvellous contrast with his outward show of vanity, and this fact made a deep impression on the old man.

Next, as the old man moved on, he was amusingly surprised to read a sign-board which struck him as making a proud display of a Kashmiri name, nay caste only preceded by its initial letters and that too so cruelly murdered by a distortion of spelling that a person who has a head on his shoulders would wonder who Mr. B.C. Cole was, an Englishman in name or in reality. Further, as he approached the Circular Road, he espied a pair of young girls, possessed of Kashmiri features, pass on bicycles talking to each other in a manner that made it difficult for him to believe his eyes.

The Kashmiri Pandit and his Panditani

Both the husband and the wife joined in holy matrimony presented the composite culture of thousands of years that Kashyp Rishi set into motion. Beginning with the nineteenth century when proper records began to be kept one gets a pen picture of how they looked, how they dressed and what kind of image they generated.

There were two distinct symbols of the traditional pandit. For his office work he would wear, as a concession to Western culture a coat and a white pyjama with traditional boots made by the cobblers in the valley. But for ensuring that his identity was recognized he wore his turban at a jaunty angle. Back at home he wore his pheran, the loose gown without the opening in front as in a Western dressing gown and pulhoru, the sandal made of grass and much later wooden clogs (called *khrave*).

While the above was the male attire the better half generally wore a loose pheran specially tailored to the women's needs and size and accompanied by a headgear (tarange) decorated appropriately to cover the head and a loose scraf tied around the waist to give her a smart look and also keep the loose dress under control while she was busy doing her domestic chores.

The march of time and the ravages of events have of course, played havoc with this visual treat of the Kashmiri pandit couple. Gone is the turban, gone is the tarange, replaced by the bare head and the hair style for the man and the pheran replaced by the saree and salwar kameez.

To the above, this writer can add: Perhaps B.C. Cole was B.C. Kaul who tried to anglicise his name. A subsequent instance can be cited. Another Kashmiri Pandit gentleman who returned from England was named Razdan. He lived on the bank of the Maer in Rainawari. He changed his name to Rozidon and named his house "Maer view." For a while, no one took notice, after a while, people laughed it away and still later people ignored it.

Members of the older generation of our community would remember the name of Pandit Lambudar Nath Zutshi, the famous mining engineer who also went to England married an Englishwoman, but never forgot his roots. My father has told me of how he would come on vacation to Kashmir and on the following day after his arrival, he would come down to the river side and greet all the Hanjis wearing a pheran and speaking chaste Kashmiri.

One has to refer from sheer necessity to the past and one would like to mention the name of Raja Narendar Nath Kaul, who was in the twenties the Revenue Minister of Jammu and Kashmir State. He belonged to the family of the Kauls of Lahore of whom one has heard a lot. There were two brothers Raja Sir Daya Kishen Kaul and Raja Hari Kishen Kaul. The latter, as most of us know, was the Prime Minister of Kashmir who put down the 1931 riots.

The story of the Raja Narendar Nath Kaul needs to be told. He was a brilliant student and had already prepared himself for the ICS for which he had to go to England. Apparently the family priests wanted him to go through some rituals. He refused. He went to England did brilliantly in the examination but failed in the horse riding Test which was compulsory. He failed because he was suffering from piles. Since he didn't qualify, he returned to India and soon after was appointed first as Governor (Deputy Commissioner) by Maharaja Hari Singh. He later became Revenue Minister.

In the following year, he chose to stay in Srinagar during winter.

Those days the valley was totally cut off from the rest of the country due to snowfall. He fell ill and had an attack of piles. Bleeding started and would not stop. The Doctors tried everything but failed and the brilliant Minister Raja Narendar Nath Koul died.

The orthodox among the Pandits ascribed his death to his lack of faith in rituals, as he did not do any after his return from England.

Orthodoxy Inc Defied

Ordhodoxy has been the bane of the Pandit community from times immemorial. Our rigidity made Renchin, a Ladhaki prince who later ruled Kashmir, convert to Islam when he wanted to become a Hindu. There were similar countless taboos. One of them was that the Pandit should not travel across the sea. What is puzzling is how this prohibition came about since many Kashmiri Pandits, Buddhist Missionaries travelled to far off places like Sri Lanka, Indonesia, China, Taiwan by sea and land.

This taboo was still in force in the nineteenth century when Pandit Mohan Lal Zutshi embarked on his adventures through many countries and became a famous explorer and helper to many British military and civil officers. He was honoured and rewarded by the British and admired by everybody in India except his own Kashmiri Pandit community. They harassed him, ex-communicated him, ostrascised him. Nobody would eat with him, nobody would invite him to his house or go to his house. In short, he was told in no uncertain terms that he was not wanted. In total frustration he converted to Islam.

In 1884, in the Kashmiri Mohalla of Lucknow, a young man named Bishan Narain Dar who lived there, broke caste restrictions against sea voyages, the news of his clandestine departure to England spread like wild fire within families living in the Mohalla, and aroused a storm of indignation, particularly among the women folk. Within a short time, a meeting of the biradari had been summoned in the shadi khana of the Kashmiri Mohalla, and an order of excommunication passed against him and his chief supporter, Pran Nath Bazaz, then a teacher in the Canning College of Lucknow.

Transition From Turban

A turban was always regarded as symbol of identity and prestige and respect. All references in our epics mention the headgear worn by Gods, Goddesses and warriors and common people. It was a part of man's standing as a male. In fact there were different kinds of turban, which identify the caste, ethnic group, profession and was a kind of ID card of an earlier era.

You may have heard of the story that emanated from the Afghan rule in Kashmir. At that time, they had passed an order that no Kashmiri Hindu could ride a horse and even those walking on the road had to keep their heads down. There was this very poor Pandit who had only one turban, which was in tatters. His resourceful wife got some colourful rags, which she stitched, together into a turban. By skillfully tying the turban he was able to hide the stitches and from the outside, it appeared to be a colourful turban.

Next day the Pandit was walking on the road to go to work when an Afghan riding a horse overtook him, liked the turban and promptly snatched the turban. But what he got in his hand was pieces of rags. He cursed and went away.

What the story highlights is that Pandits were poor as a community but they did not lack in ingenuity, innovation, and patience. That is how they survived.

Reverting to turbans, in the early part of the twentieth century, even young boys studying in class 3 or 4 were required to wear turbans. There is an old photograph showing a group of students in the Mission School in the 1890s. in which all Biscoe's students of practically all the classes wore turbans.

When a person took up a job, he had to wear a turban. Even policemen wore khaki turbans. Thus it was that my father and my uncle wore turbans. While my father was modern in his tastes, my uncle was always traditional, orthodox with a minimum of modern accompaniments. Till the day he passed away, he wore his traditional turban. But my father deserted the tradition in 1948 during his first posting outside the state and remained turban less till they day he died.

The above is a glimpse of headgear but for the rest most of the Pandits switched to European clothing and it was till very recently that the unspoken convention of wearing a necktie was confined only to gazetted officers. Even now, one can find in Kashmir non-gazetted officers not wearing a tie and moving around in just a coat and a pant.

Faith and Belief

The Father was worried. The son was going on a long journey. He briefed him, advised him, gave suggestions for safety. He helped him to pack and finally asked him.

"Any questions?"

"Yes, what do I do if my holy thread breaks or gets lost?"

"Well, It's written in our Shastras that in an emergency you can take any piece of string, say a prayer over it and it gets consecrated. After that, you can put it on and it becomes your holy thread."

"What if I cannot get a piece of string. Then what do I do?"

It is provided in our shastras that in that case you can dip your fingers into water and draw a line along the same line on which the real thread would hang.

What do I do if there is no water?

Then, my son," sighed the father," ONLY GOD CAN HELP YOU.

The Way Things Were

Even today, there is no sewage in Srinagar City especially the old city of Seven bridges and areas surrounding it and linking it to Rainawari. Of course, in the past fifty years since Independence new extensions like Bal Garden, Magarmal Bagh and other areas do have sewage but the old areas still live in primitive conditions. Most of them have now pits since the profession of picking up night soil has practically disappeared not only in Kashmir valley but also in the rest of India.

The first experience that Srinagar city had of modern housing was the development of Karan Nagar (named after Yuvaraj Karan Singh). This is located beyond Kani Kadal across the main road and was popularly known as Dewan Bagh. Quite a few progressive well to do Pandits built their houses there. This was perhaps the first middle class locality and it was half way towards the rich and the super rich living near Dal Gate and on Gupkar road.

The strange thing, looking at it at this distance of time, is that houses did not even have Municipal numbers. They were identified largely by the owners' names. When electric meters were installed after the arrival of electricity, the billing was only by the name of the owner and the localities name, either the Mohalla or the Kocha (Lane).

As recently as the eighties I have addressed letters where only the name of the person and the locality and its proximity to the relevant number of the bridge is written. For instance:

Prof. N.L. Darbari
Narpirastan, 2nd Bridge,
Srinagar, Kashmir.

As you can see from the above, this is not an accurate address. Mind you, Narpirastan is closer to the Third Bridge than to the Second Bridge. But the reason why the letters reached their destination is because the Postman from the second bridge (Haba Kadal) served our Mohalla.

The location of people and houses was also a beautifully romantic, vague system, which surprisingly enough worked. The following conversation will illustrate it:

> Can you tell me the way to Prof. Wazir's House?
>
> Go straight towards Habba Kadal beyond Chinkral Mohalla. You will find Dr.Sham Bhat's House. It is just practically opposite. In fact it is on the main road

So the key identification mark is Sham Bhat. Who was he? The late Pandit Sham Bhat was a respected doctor who was well known to all Pandits in Srinagar and beyond. Thus, the man looking for a particular address in that locality would be told the approximate distance and direction that house was in relation to the good Doctor's house. The main method of identification was first and foremost with regard to addresses the proximity of the bridge on the river Jhelum. It had to be either between second and third bridge or fourth and sixth bridge.

Earlier, we mentioned Prof. Darbari. Suppose, I was giving instructions to someone to go to his house. I would say "From

Maalik Aangan walk a little further and you will come on the main road to the shrine of Narishwari where there is a lamp lit and beyond it is a Mazar. Next to it, is a Lane. On the other side of it is a "Kandar Waan " (Pandit Baker). Go through the lane until you reach the Kachroo House and then watch out for another Lane going to Razdan Kocha, but keep going. On the left side you will find the Darbari House.

What is this X-Ray?

Modern Medicine came to Kashmir valley through the good offices of the medical missionaries of the CMS of London. The Neve brothers were both doctors and the mission hospital that they set up can still be seen there today as we go through the twenty-first century. One of the greatest diagnostic tools of modern medicine was the x-ray and what Srinagar city, the main urban hub of the Kashmir valley, lacked was the newly developed x-ray machine, which had been commercialized in Europe in the early 30s and had come to commercial centers in India. The nearest big centre for the Kashmir valley was Lahore (now in Pakistan)

It was at this juncture that a Kashmiri Pandit doctor decided to set up his x-ray clinic in the valley. Until then, there was no facility for the general public to have an x-ray taken. This was Dr. Shivji Dhar who started a clinic for x-rays and today much more than half a century later, it is still there despite wars, terrorism, militancy and natural calamities.

This was a pioneering effort by a member of the community, which is basically a service-oriented community. Dr. Shivji Dhar's grandson Dr. Hiralal Dhar, a medical graduate of the Madras University, is today running it very efficiently.

Spring Time, Picnic Time

It was a period of transition. Electric light had made its appearance but it was not universal. Cars were few; there was no public transport. Most people depended on their legs and for longer distances it was the horse drawn carriage known as the Tonga. Radio was rare and movies had just come but were taboo as going to the movies was considered to be something bad.

Under these circumstances, how did the people amuse themselves? What we call fun today was also there but in a different form. Enjoyment was also dictated by, strange as it may sound now, the seasons. After the hellish winter was over and spring had come, it was time to picnic. The most famous picnic of the season was "Badamwari." A word of explanation.

Almond trees initially have flowers, which bloom in spring, and groves and groves of it with fresh grass growing on the ground provided the ideal local for a picnic. Most families would pack up their samavars and sweets and other eatables and carry them to these badamwaris where they would sit on the ground and enjoy the scenery.

The children, practically imprisoned during the six months of winter, suddenly discovered the joy of freedom and one could hear shouting, screaming and playing all over the picnic grounds. The adults would sit and quite often meet some others whom they would not have seen during the winter.

It was the beginning of the new year and a change from the day-to-day drudgery of work both for the men as well as the women.

As the spring advanced into summer and the Mughal gardens adjoining the Dal Lake were opened up for visitors, the locals mixed with the tourists who were also coming to Nishat, Shalimar and Harwan to name just a few.

How did the locals go for such a picnic?

Whereas they walked to badamwari, Nishat was a bit far away. The journey was conducted by riding the native boat called a dhoonga. It has to be borne in mind that when such an outing was planned terrific, excitement prevailed especially among the children. Women would plan the menu and select their best pots and pans including the inseparable samavar. They would board the dhoonga at the nearest point on the Jhelum river and it would either be an overnight trip or, as was the case mostly, a one day trip beginning with the departure early in the morning and arrival late at night.

For the Pandits, there were places where they went on pilgrimage such as Amarnath, Ishibar, Mattan, Verinag and Khirbhavani. While Amarnath was a tough three-week trip, Khirbavani (Tulla mula) was the most popular. Here too, the journey was made by dhoonga and in most cases it was an overnight trip. Khirbhavani was a perennial destination as one could go there at any time. However the festival associated with the shrine is Jeth Ashtami.

Exodus

By the mid fifties it was quite clear that employment opportunities within the state would keep on shrinking because there would be more Muslim candidates for any Government job. In order to satisfy the aspirations of Kashmiri Muslims, the Government of J&K declared education from Class I to M.A. level free, although it was not the post 1947 Government which did it, but the Government of Maharaja Hari Singh which made education practically free. Even today it is the only state in India, which has free education all through.

During the thirties and forties, a few Pandits had ventured into the field of Engineering and Medicine. And after Independence, when a tremendous expansion of developmental activities was planned for the whole country, Kashmir also got its share.

The first crop of youngsters all wanted to become civil engineers but most of them could not get admission into the degree (B.E) course. So they went in for the next best thing, the diploma course which qualified them for an overseer's job. With fresh projects coming in a steady stream, overseers had no problem finding jobs and brides.

This was a period when the Overseer was highly prized as a potential or future son-in-law in the marriage market. The conversation between illiterate women of the older generation and middle-aged women with some education was revealing to the extent that one could gauge a change in the value system in the community.

- What is the boy doing?
- He has just joined the PWD as an Overseer
- What is his salary?
- Salary is only one fifty, but over that he gets *Phetwain,* meaning thereby extra money from other sources or as they say in Hindi "Ghoos."

The sixties and seventies saw a gradual movement of young men who could not get a seat in the newly opened Engineering colleges and the Medical Colleges in the State. Most of them studied outside, qualified and took up a job wherever they could get it. Of course, their parents stayed back and they would visit the valley in summer and spend the leave there.

Gradually, avenues of employment in the state dried up and practically every young boy knew that he would have to leave the state for acquiring a technical or professional qualification. This went on right during the eighties until they were thrown out by murder and torture in 1989-90.

Gradually the preference for civil engineering died out and many opted for other branches and today (2005) quite a large number have opted for computer related subjects like software and electronics etc.

Earlier recruits in Jammu & Kashmir Government retired and were replaced by Muslims. Apart from this, more and more exposure to Punjab, Delhi, Bombay, Calcutta, Hyderabad, Bangalore, Pune and Chennai broadened the outlook but also physically scattered the community. Though a number of associations were founded and are working quite well, the exodus from Kashmir has had its effect in further splintering the community.

Building a House — A Lifetime Achievement

Under any circumstances, building a house in India is most of the time a once in a lifetime activity. What you build in this generation is generally bequeathed to the next generation as an inheritance.

There was this Pandit whose wife was pestering him to build a house. After marshalling his resources, he finally agreed and already owning the land, he felt it would not be such a costly undertaking. In those days, No architect was employed and the plan was simple and straightforward - ground floor kitchen and living room, first floor bedroom and second floor summer living room.

Generally speaking, in Srinagar in every Mohalla one could find a mid wife, a compounder, a carpenter, a mason, a baker, a grocer, a milkman, a vegetable seller etc. Once the decision was made, the local mason was contacted and, to cut a long story short, construction began.

The first payment had to be made before construction and the second payment after the foundation was laid. Every day, after the construction began, the owner used to come directly from the office and watch the final stages of the day's work.

It was a sight to see. The pride in his eyes, the gestures for the neighbours and the pose that would put a Raj Kapoor to shame. And in filmi style, he would take out his packet of Gold Flake and light up a cigarette, blowing rings of smoke into the air.

Very soon, the walls for the first floor began to be built and more money was needed for which he tried to take a Provident Fund loan. Naturally, paper work, especially in a

Government Office, takes time and even if it is meant for a Government Employee it still takes time. Hence, our hero was worried. The mason, the carpenter, the labourers, the cement, the woodwork had all to be paid for and they had not yet reached the first floor.

The money came, the pressing bills were paid, but money seemed to be in short supply and he had to come down from Gold Flake to Cavendar. Anyway the wife was happy the house was coming up and she was looked upon with envy by the rest of the ladies in the locality.

But the master of the house was worried, terribly worried. He began to wear a pinched look on his face. It seemed to him the second phase of the construction was going painfully slow and his money was running out faster than the house was coming up. Eventually, the first floor was also completed and by the time they reached the second floor our hero's money ran out but he was one of those who never say die.

(The expression is, "he never says die" that is, he never gives up)

The head mason was laying the bricks for the wall and his assistant was helping him. He took a break to have a smoke and was talking softly to his assistant.

"Have you noticed that he has changed to Cavendar and I guarantee you that next month he will change to Red Lamp."

"I do not think so," said the younger man and added, "He is not that poor"

"We will see."

And sure enough, in two weeks time, our hero came down to Red Lamp, which was of course, to cheapest brand of cigarette in that Golden Era of the twentieth century.

But our Pandit hero finally built the house and lived happily ever after in it, that is, until Pakistan's export of terrorism hit the Valley in 1989.

Byon Nerun (Family Partition)

It was only in the twenties and thirties that the population increased and with education, old social taboos began to crack. Family fights resulting from differences between father and son, mother-in-law and daughter-in-law resulted in expected acrimony and in a few cases the partition of the family took place.

As years went by and the economic condition of the community improved, partition became less painful but what we are talking about here is division of an old house and separation of generally the kitchen and the bed rooms.

Very often, the acrimony would begin in two areas after the partition — one is sharing of the water tap and the other that of the toilet. In our neighbourhood also, such a partition took place and where one kitchen would feed a family of ten, two kitchens would feed four on one side and six on the other. Thus, the beginning of the modern age started, where individual comfort started becoming more and more important and convenience for the younger generations became more important, came. However, the blame for partition has been, I feel, wrongly placed at the door of the young daughter-in-law who is branded as the villain who turns her husband against his parents.

This is however a glance at the past. Happily enough today family partitions are no longer acrimonious.

Batta* Tongawalla

He was a young man full of hope, energy and enthusiasm. But his parents were poor. He passed his High School and started looking for a job. He looked and looked and looked but there was no job.

He was desperate. One day a neighbour in the Mohalla asked him to help bring his horse from the barn and harness

---

* Batta, Kashmiri word for Kashmiri Pandits.

it to the *tonga,* which he was driving. After thanking our boy, he asked whether he would like to drive a tonga and earn some money. Our boy was desperate and he said Yes.

And so began his journey into the unknown world of Batta (Pandit) Prejudice. Even as he tried the new job, he found he liked it. It was difficult, it was hard work but it had its rewards. At the end of the day, he had money. He was afraid to tell his parents at home about his new job. But one day they found out and told him to stop.

What will the neighbours say? They have given us a new name. They call us *Tongawalla.*

He argued himself hoarse pointing out that if he had another job, he would not certainly drive a *tonga.* Suddenly, he decided to become obstinate. He refused to give it up. He did the job, earned the money and saved some. By this time, everybody called him a Tongawalla. Especially those from the KP community. But he did not care.

He left the Valley, learned to drive a car and lived happily ever after. This is one story. There is another one (and many more) about our prejudice with regard to professions, which are not socially acceptable.

There were two Young men - Somnath and Janakinath. Both were interested in hairdressing. They were promptly nicknamed Barbers (Navid) but again they were determined, left the valley and went to Bombay where they made good and lived happily ever after.

Social attitudes have changed but a lot more needs changing.

The Three Rs and Eve

As late as the 1920s, very few girls were sent to school or college. A few used to be sent to primary or to middle school level and then brought home and prepared for their marriage. In our own joint family, the first two girls, one born in the twenties and other in the thirties, were educated only upto the primary level, whereas the third daughter born in the forties was lucky to get a good education.

One of the main reasons for this was first physical safety and second lack of avenues of employment after education. Also the overriding factor was that the qualitative requirement for a bride in the twenties, thirties and forties was ability in house work rather than education. Among the more orthodox a girl who went to school was considered to be a risk so far as character was concerned.

After Independence, as avenues of employment within the valley decreased and mobility gradually took hold, the Pandit boys were educated at the school level and up to the intermediate level in the valley after which most of them went to other parts of India for pursuing technical courses as Medicine or Post-graduate studies in universities. Simultaneously, with this, the number of schools and colleges for women increased within the Valley and this gave an opportunity for the Pandit girls to study beyond high school and even in professional courses. This trend started in the fifties and continued up to the seventies by which time practically every Pandit family had a relative outside the Valley, which made it easy for either a boy or a girl to go and persue higher studies outside Kashmir.

By the time the eighties came round, all children whether boys or girls had to have an education even in those families which were located in villages or some towns like Khanabal, Anantnag, Baramulla, Sopore, Kupwara, Verinag, Mattan etc., Today, no one even asks whether the girl is educated or not because everyone takes it for granted that she will be educated at least up to the degree level.

It is for this reason one can safely say that the half a million Kashmiri Pandit community scattered all round India and around the world is a hundred percent literate community.

In most Hindu communities in India, there has always been dowry present in some form or the other Kashmir is no exception. In Kashmir according to their status, dowry would be paid but it was never called dowry since, we had an ancient code of conduct and even a graded slab system of payment of money or giving of presents on various occasions in terms of cash or kind. This has been graphically described by Pandit Anand Kaul in his pioneering work, *"The Kashmiri Pandit"* published in 1924.

Marconi Comes to Kashmir

Radio had come to Kashmir but was mainly used for military purposes, by the Maharaja and other important people of the state. Its actual sale in a shop began in 1946 after the war.

In the words of Mr. J.L. Ganjoo (*Koshur Samachar*, August 2001), his father Pandit Niranjan Nath Ganjoo bought a radio set on July 5th, 1946. A limited quantity had come to Kashmir for sale and this was perhaps the first indroduction of Kashmiris to radio as a medium of news and entertainment.

The Kashmiri Pandit is famous for hospitality. Pay a visit to him and he will treat you to the point of worship. It is not uncommon that he will offer food prepared for himself to a guest who chances to come unexpectedly to his house and will himself remain hungry until fresh food is prepared for him. If a guest comes to his house and he has got no cash at hand with which to buy tea to be served to him, he will secretly go and pawn one of his personal effects and bring the tea. Well, someone has said:

Zara zara hai mere Kashmir ka mihman-nawaz
Rah men pthar ke tukrun se mila pani mujhe.

Everywhere greets me the hospitable host of my Kashmir.
I got water from even the pebbles on the way.

The Pandit is intelligent. Even at a distance in the Durbar he can tell by observing the movements of the Secretary's pen what orders are being dictated by the Maharaja. Aurangzeb once paid a compliment to his intelligence at Agra as is recorded in the *Ruqat-I-Alamgiri*:

> *Kashmiri darin mulk nistand ki ma muqurar kunem*
> The Kashmiris are not to be found here, that we might appoint them in public offices.

He is shrewd, alive to the comic touch, and has a natural gift of repartee. During the Pathan rule a Pandit was asked by a Sirdar why there were 108 beads in the rosary round his neck. "Because the beads are used to keep count in the recitation of the name of Haw (God)," was the ready reply, "the two letters of H and Q standing as they are for 108 in reckoning by *abjad*." Diwan Dila Ram Quili Khan was once sarcastically asked by Timur Shah Durani at Kabul why the tika mark was made by him on his forehead. He replied that it indicated that God was one. Timur Shah enquired why the ears were also marked. He explained that it was to show that they were two witnesses to this fact. Timur Shah, in order to baffle him, further asked why the throat was also besmeared. He replied that it meant that whoever entertained any doubt about it was fit to be beheaded. The King was pleased with the plausibility of the answers to his questions and then Dila Ram Quli Khan bore the bell by adding the following two couplets in Persian:

> *Bar chahra am nazar kum peshaniam bibin*
> *Dagha ghulamia Shahi-Maulasi bar jebin*
> *Gar Musalman Kafir o Kafir Musalman shud chi shud*
> *Ancha bayad shud no shud gar in u gar an shud chi shud.*
> Look at my face and see my forehead
> The mark of slavery of the Master King is on my forehead
> If Musalman became a Kafir or Kafir a Musalman
> If he did not become what he ought to (i.e., pious, God fearing, etc.)
> What matters it if he became this (Kafir) or that (Musalman).

Low Profile

Because of continuous persecution by Muslim Rulers for almost 500 years, the Pandits who survived the onslaught of forcible conversions made it a policy to maintain a low profile, which over the generations became a part of the Pandit psyche.

This would be reflected in the behaviour of the majority of the Pandits most of whom were clerks. They were very few senior officers who were Pandits and the number of rich men, landlords, and businessman could be counted on one's fingers.

The watchword was "Don't come to the notice of the rulers or don't become prominent or don't do anything that makes you stand out in a crowd." This perhaps is responsible for two proverbs, which are typical of the community. One is "He was born under this quilt and he died under the same quilt."

It is the second, one, which needs elaboration, It is **"Nav Zanehemne Kahn."** Literally translated it means it "Nobody knew my name". This would explain the need for anonymity among the Pandits. To stay unseen and be part of the crowd.

As a twelve-year-old schoolboy,in Madras where prohibition was in force, I did not know what the word "Beer" meant. Somebody in my father's office asked me to find out whether this commodity would be available from the parents of any of my classmates in the English School that I was studying in. I faithfully carried out the task and the next day somebody came and met my father asking him whether he wanted beer.

After cross questioning the gentleman who was the father of one of my classmates, my father found out that the entire conspiracy had started with one of his own subordinates in the office. So when I came during the lunch hour, he closed the office door and gave me the thrashing of my life.

It is not the thrashing that I remember, but what he said. I had by associating myself with beer defamed him and brought down his prestige. The famous last words that still keep ringing in my ears were and are:

"Nav Zanehemne Kahn" (None knew my name. By implication my bad deed would give him a bad name. Stems from the Pandits psyche to keep a low profile all the time and not come to the notice of other people)

"Our Lone Industrialist"

By the early forties, English had completely seeped into the community as an essential basic ingredient to advancement in life. And the word industrialist meant very little as most of us, especially the adults, who had rarely been outside the State, but familiarity with the English language gave a vague idea that an industrialist was a big business man no matter what his business was.

So it came about that by then the name of Pandit Jawaharlal Nehru and his link with the Kashmiri Pandits and his leadership of the Congress party came as a surprise initially since he had been an exile whose family had left the Valley as a result of religious persecution.

He came to visit the Valley, and the local Pandits gave him a reception and invited him to visit the interior part of Srinagar. As he was being given a guided tour, one of his hosts proudly pointed to a small building on the road in Bana Mohalla and said, "Sir, that is his factory." And pointing to a smiling stout gentleman he added with great pride, "Sir, and he is our only industrialist."

Nehru smiled nodded and shook the hand of the industrialist and passed on down the street.

The factory that was shown to him was a rice mill and the industrialist who was introduced to him was Pandit Jia Lal Khod, the nice kindly man, who for no fault of his, was pushed forward by eager do-gooders.

Today we have quite a few top business experts and leaders who started out as executives and made a name for themselves in the world of business. For instance A.N. Haksar, J.N. Sapru, Rajive Kaul, Dr. R.N. Kar, A.N. Dhar, V.K. Dhar, M.L. Zutshi, Mohan Lal Shishoo, Hira Lal Zutshi and many others. But even in this area, Pandits shine more as consultants, business executives and employees.

The greatest Social Reformer produced by the Kashmiri Pandit community, Pandit Kashyap Bandhu, persuaded gently the womenfolk to give up the old, cumbersome, dress called Pheran. Although it was pretty to look at, it restricted movement . He resorted to folk poetry and following is the poem in Kashmiri with English translation that gave a clarion call to Pandits to modernize or be left behind:

1. Travee Pheran lo lo	**Give up Pheran, O dear**
2. Zooj, Pooch tye nariwar	**Zooj, Pooch and nariwar**
3. Yim chhi Shikasik Sardar	**These are agents of degradation**
4. Mala barhaiy gardun	**These have filled your neck with dirt**
5. Travee Pheran lo lo	**Give up Pheran, O dear**
6. Pooch Pathkun Pakan	**Pooch drags you backwards**
7. Walna Yiwan Zangan,	**It envelops your legs**
8. Chanda Sadkan doova	**The hanging pocket (attached to your Pheran) is sweeping roads.**
9. Travee Pheran lo lo	**Give up Pheran, O dear**
10. Tarang Chhuee akh Khara	**Your headwear tarang is as heavy as a ton**

11. Kalas Peth bodh barah	**It is a heavy load on your head**
12. Vank Panuk Soodh Kyah? hanging through our back?	**What is the use of long hair tail hanging through your back?**
13. Zethem Ziuth lotach, Asan Janvaran	**Which is attached to animals.**
14. Travi Pheran lo lo	**Give up Pheran, O dear**

6

The Biscoe Age

In All Things be Men

REV. Tyndale Biscoe wrote three books relating to his 57 years life in the Kashmir Valley from 1890 to 1947. The first one was *"Kashmir In Sunlight and Shade"*, published in 1922. The second one was *"Men in the making"*, while the third one, his autobiography entitled *"Biscoe of Kashmir — an autobiography."* This was published soon after his death on August 1, 1948 at Salisbury (Harare) in Rhodesia (now Zimbabwe).

The following pages contain excerpts from both these books about Bisoce Sahib's lifelong crusade in Kashmir.

Remembering Biscoe

The only reminder of teacher, educationist, guide, friend, philosopher and man Tyndale Biscoe in Kashmir, apart from the six Mission Schools, today is the fluency with which Kashmiris speak, read, write and even teach English that has now graduated from being the mother tongue of the Englishman to that of being an international language.

He not only brought English to the Valley, which opened the window to the world for the Kashmiris, but also discipline and qualities which he imparted to his thousands of students, which is aptly enshrined in the school motto "In all things be men".

In every state in India, there have been selfless Englishmen who have served India by teaching, learning and giving.

Grateful people have not forgotten them. In almost every case, State Governments honoured the educationists, scholars and professionals in practically every walk of life, who were Englishmen, part of the Raj, but selfless and devoted in their integrity and sevice.

But Kashmir has not done any such thing. There is no fellowship, scholarship, no state honour for the man who brought Kashmir into the twentieth century, made Kashmir is aware of the world around them and gave them modern knowledge, taught them compassion, dignity of labour and blending the body physical with the the soul and producing a wholesome likeable man or women.

The only sign of respect and regard for him was put up by his grateful students in the form of a small statue of his which was installed at the east side of the newly built Fateh Kadal near DiwanTemple. Even this was defaced and mutilated.

Today, a considerable portion of the State Revenue comes from tourism. It was Biscoe who developed the awareness among Kashmiris, the rest of Indians and Europeans, and foreigners of the beauty of Kashmir and the ability to appreciate it. In fact, he was in a way, the father of modern tourism in Kashmir.

Whatever tourist spots are being encashed by the Tourism Department of Jammu and Kashmir are all discoveries of Biscoe, namely, Neel Naag, Kaunsernaag, Ahrabal Falls, Dacchegam, Kolahai, Mahadev, Zabarwan and many more.

Kashmir has forgotten Biscoe, but Biscoe's disciples have not forgotten him. It is sad that for a man who gave so much to Kashmir, Kashmir has given nothing in return. He spent 57 years of his life in selfless service for Kashmir. Even his name has been forgotten. Sad and pathetic. A case of extreme ingratitude.

Teacher Comes to Town

Canon Cecil Tyndale Biscoe was born in 1863 in a family with one daughter and seven sons. He graduated in 1886 from Cambridge University and was ordained as priest and appointed in the Bradfield Parish.

In 1890, he was selected by the Church Missionary Society (CMS), London, to go to Kashmir and help Rev.H.J.Knowels at his school in Fateh Kadal ,Srinagar, Kashmir. In November 1890, he arrived in Srinagar and initially stayed with the two famous Medical Missionary brothers Dr. Arthur and Ernest Neve who set up the Mission Hospital in Srinagar.

Boat Club

> On arrival in Kashmir in 1891, I found that the European community had a boat club. Colonel Sartorius, V.C., who was secretary, was leaving Kashmir, so I was asked to take his place and build some more rowing boats. Although I knew very little about building boats, I thought I might at any rate have to learn. So, with the help of some friends who did know how to build boats, I superintended the work of carpenters who built them.
>
> —Tyndale Biscoe, *Kashmir In Sunlight & Shade*, 1922.

Swimming is also education (1893)

This happened in 1893. Here are two instances where persuasion was needed. One of the principal Ministers of Kashmir requested me to prepare his son for Oxford University. He had already passed matriculation of the Punjab University.

I said that I would accept this responsibility on three conditions; one, he would pay the tuition fee in advance, two, he would permit me to teach him manners and three that I might teach him to swim. To these three conditions, he agreed. So I said: Send him along.

"Most Respected Sir, — I most humbly and respectfully beg to bring to your kind notice that my son, Siri Bhan, student of the Lower School, is strictly prohibited by astrologers, who have examined his horoscope, from joining any playing party, etc. I would request you to kindly keep him exempt from joining the playing teams and boating, etc. I beg to remain, etc."

Comment: If swimming was dangerous, God would not have created rivers.

Tyndale Biscoe, *Kashmir In Sunlight & Shade*, 1922

At 7.30 a.m. he arrived at my house in good spirits, saying that he was ready for work. "That is good," I said, "but where is the tuition fee?" "My father will send it. He is a rich man." "That I know very well," said I, hence my desire to see the money in advance. "No money, no tuition, so off you run for the money." I had previously had money transactions with his father.

Within half an hour, he was back with a bag of rupees, which I counted to see that all was square — no counterfeit coins. Fortunately for him, all was correct. Manners, also satisfactory as payment had been prompt. Now for the third condition; lesson in swimming. "We will start at once for the lake." To that, he took strong exception, saying: "Sir, I cannot learn to swim. I am not a coolie, I am a gentleman." "That is interesting" said I. "Suppose you and your mother were walking by the side of the river and she fell in, what would you do?"

"Oh! I would call a coolie and send him in after her." "But suppose there was no coolie, what would you do?" To this question he had no reply ready.

So I said: "Mount your bicycle. We must start for the lake at once." We had gone only half a mile when he called out: Sahib, please stop, my bicycle is punctured." This was a fact, as he had been riding behind me, and jumped off, and certainly had punctured his tyre. "No matter," I replied, "just shove your cycle against the fence and we will walk the mile and a half to the lake." We did this, the son of this very rich Minister, although a "gentleman" received his first lessons.

Mission School boys saved 400 people from drowning. This is a record in the valley and the Mission School was the first to make swimming compulsory and life saving a part of the curriculum. The saddest part of that is that out of 400 boys whose lives were saved, only the parents of two boys came to thank the school, or the principal or the headmaster or the boys who actually saved their children from drowning.

"Later on, I saw the boy at Cambridge. He was then cox of one of the Trinity boats and most thankful that he could swim like all the members of his college 'coolie' crew."

Years passed, the son now an M.A., of Cambridge, and L.L.B. of Dublin as well, was back in his own country in an important position with His Highness the Maharajah of Jammu and Kashmir. In many ways, he helped the schools when in difficulty. He had become a gentleman, indeed!

Birdwood (1919)

> Our annual swim this year across the Dal Lake was a red letter day for us. At the place on the lake side from where our boys were starting on their swim was a small encampment. Out of one of the tents came a British Officer who asked me what I was doing, and when I told him that the boys were going to swim across the lake, he became very interested and asked if he might join them. I told him that of course we should be honoured if he would take part.
>
> He went into the tent and was soon out again in bathing kit and swam off with the boys. I asked another officer who he was. He replied: "General Sir William Birdwood, the Commander-in-Chief." I had not recognized him, as it was over thirty years since I had met this delightful soldier. I am glad to say that it was not the last. The general did not

realize what valuable help he was giving us for he was not aware of the attitude of the Kashmiris towards swimming and sport.

At this particular time, there were over a hundred boys attempting the long swim and not one of their parents had bothered to come to see them, whereas here was the C-in-C. of India joining the Kashmir boys in this swimming contest.

General Birdwood was responsible for setting up the Indian Military Academy (IMA) which opened in 1932. The first batch which passed out from the I.M.A included Field Marshal Sam Manekshaw.

— Tyndale Biscoe of Kashmir, *An autobiography*, 1949

Carpentry and Pandits (1898)

In 1898, our school staff now looked like a family affair, with Augustus Tyndale plus my brother George. L. Estrange was a wrangler and was a great help in instructing our staff in higher mathematics, and Augustus an M.A. keen on history, and a proficient carpenter. We soon had a carpentry shop to help conquer the prejudice against carpentry as we had conquered opposition against football, boxing, swimming and much else. Also the carpentry in Kashmir as regards furniture was bad, glue and nails being used instead of mortices. In fact, furniture was just knocked together.

Dignity of Labour (1901)

One of the first carpenter Brahmanas to face the anger of the Orthodox Brahman's is still living (1947) and is one of the best furniture makers in Kashmir; not only has he learnt to be a master carpenter, but he has learnt to laugh. When we took him on, we could not persuade him even to smile; he had a perpetual scowl. Augustus cured him and later he became carpenter instructor to British schoolboys.

Educating Pandits was a mistake (1903)

On one of my visits outside the V.alley, I first went to Delhi and from there to the delightful home of Colonel George Strahan at Dehra Doon. The Colonel was a great landscape painter. When I went into his studio he said: "Please take any paintings you like." I chose one of Pahalgam, because his tent was in the foreground where I had visited him about 10 years back when recovering from typhoid. He was the first Britisher who showed any interest in our schools or wished me God speed. The Sahibs in those days thought that by educating the Kashmiris we were making a mistake; that an educated thief is more dangerous than an uneducated one. They could, or would not, believe that we were character building and not interested in turning out just B.A., and failed B.A.s.

Head Master Shankar Koul (1907)

"What Shankar does not know is not worth knowing"

My Punjabi Christian Head Master asked for a year's leave, which I granted. As I needed a man in his place, I put an advertisement in the *Civil and Military Gazette, Lahore* as follows: "Wanted a headmaster for the C.M.S. schools in Kashmir; no one with proud look or high stomach need apply to the Rev.C.E. Tyndale Biscoe.

By return of post, I received a postcard from the Head of the Cambridge Mission in Delhi, saying: "We have all been very sorry to see your advertisement in the Civil and Military Gazette, for you have upset the whole of Delhi." That was a bad business! But nevertheless, I received seventy applications for the post. But I could accept not one, for I could see by their letters that they had high stomachs and I guessed that proud looks were above these stomachs. So failing to find a suitable man from the colleges in India, I appointed one of our staff, Mr. Shankar Koul, who remained our headmaster for forty years, a record.

No school could have had a more capable leader of boys and a more loyal worker. A very successful teacher in the classroom, but as a leader in all social services for the welfare of his country, he was superb. From being a leader in preventing cruelty to animals, he tackled a far greater evil, cruelty to women. Out of the hundreds of instances of tackling cruelties to animals I will mention an amusing one.

I was standing in the school compound and happened to look at the entrance gate, which was under an arch, when lo and behold, a pair of donkey's ears appeared, so high up that they could hardly pass under the arch. Then gradually, as this apparition came into fuller view, I perceived that a donkey was riding on man's back, its forelegs sticking out over the man's chest. Shankar Koul then explained that as he came to school, he saw a little donkey doing its best to carry a man nearly as big as itself, so he thought it better that the man should carry the donkey. He made the two change places, in fairness to the donkey.

Head Master Sridhar Bhat, Anantnag (1914)

A boy called Shridar Bhat came to the school and, in course of time, became headmaster. He possessed an outstanding character for courage, kindness and determination and his great joy in life was that of uplifting the Kashmiris.

Whilst he was a master in the school, a lady missionary, Miss Annie Coverdale, started a school for girls. She and Shridhar Bhat did everything they could for each other's schools. If anyone congratulated Shrider Bhat on his success with his school and in social service, he always said it is all due to Miss Coverdale's example and help.

Miss Coverdale lived with Dr. Minny Gomery and Miss Katie Newnham at the C.M.S mission hospital at Anantnag. They had devoted their lives to the women of this town and district for years. It was most strenuous work and we all marvelled at their strength and courage. Miss Coverdale eventually retired to England but was unfortunately one of the many victims in an air raid. She and her sister's cottage at

Bexhill received a direct hit from a bomb. In the hereafter, many will call her blessed.

Election of Shankar Koul to the Municipal Council (1916)

At this time, the city of Srinagar was excited over its Municipal election. Our headmaster, Mr. Shankar Koul, was asked to stand and was naturally backed up by all who wished to have an honest municipal officer. When our masters and old boys presented themselves at the election booths, they found it impossible to vote as the municipal secretary was there with hooligans to prevent them voting, so we had to send some lusty fellows to see fair play, and Mr. Shankar Koul was duly elected.

Now I would like you to know something of the life and character of Mr. Shankar Koul our Headmaster, who was now an honourable member of the municipality of Srinagar. He came to the mission school in 1892 together with two boys from the state school. Their first half-morning's work was finished when the bell rang for them to go into the playground for the twenty minutes' exercise, drill, boxing and gymnastics.

When I ordered my class to shut their books and to go the playground, these three new boys said that they had come to school to learn and not to play. So I told them that this school was not a lunatic asylum and that, if they did not wish to have their bodies trained, they had better return at once to the state school. I then forced them downstairs to the playground and put them in line with the squad fronting the parallel bars and, when their turn came to perform, they refused to mount the parallel bars. So I took out my watch and told them that I would give them five minutes to think the matter over and then something would happen. Something did happen. Shankar Koul was on the parallel bars but his arms were too weak to hold himself there, so two boys were called to support him on each side.

When this first exercise was finished, we dealt with the other two newcomers in the same way. All three boys accepted this treatment with good grace, and, later on, all three became gymnastic instructors and thankful that they had come to the school.

To speak of Shankar Koul's life at the C.M.S schools and the enormous amount of useful work and brave deeds that he has performed would fill volumes. He was the leader of the boys at fires in the city, at epidemics of cholera, and when the Jhelum river overflowed its banks, causing destruction and distress all around. He was in the vanguard too in preventing cruelty to animals, and in rescuing women and girls from impure devils. He also did useful work in standing up to the state officials when they tried to harm our schools and was always ready to join battle with anyone who decried the school.

By July 1899, The Mission School had 44 Kashmiri teachers (in those days they were called masters). Three of them were Christians, five were Muslims 36 were Kashmiri Pandits. Nearly all of them were old boys of the Mission Schools where they had studied under the supervision of Tyndale Biscoe. They all worked loyally for much less pay than they would have got in Government service.

Wular Lake Challenge (1929)

I now come to an important event, the first swimming of the dreaded Wular Lake, which at its narrowest point was five miles wide. About ten years previously, I had taken the twelve-oared cutter with a crew of twelve Brahman, teachers and a few passengers to introduce them to the joys of boating.

The Kashmiris are terribly frightened of the Wular Lake on account of storms that now and again blow up. As all the boats are flat-bottomed, not built to face storms, they often capsize and the crews and passengers, being non-swimmers, are drowned. These deaths are supposed to be caused by djinns, or the god of the lake.

We had not left the shore many minutes when a breeze sprang up and the boat began to heel over and toss a little. This put the "wind up" those on board and they started to call out to their gods, Ram and Shiva. Some quite lost their heads and began to weep, thinking of their loved ones at home safe on terra firma whom they would never see again. They threw out handfuls of rice and sugar as baksheesh to their gods. I am afraid, I was unsympathetic and, like Elijah of old, told them to cry aloud to their gods, for perchance they slept. In a short while, the god of the lake had pity on them, the wind dropped and our boat was soon on an even keel. We took to our oars and were shortly at our destination across the lake.

Arrived there, we found much stir among the people, who told us that the day before there had been a heavy storm and eighteen fishermen had been drowned. On my asking why they had not swum ashore, they said that no one around the lake could save their lives by swimming for the djinns always pulled them under the water, so what was the use of learning to swim. Our school teachers seemed much upset at this tragedy, so I said to them: "Don't you think that it is up to us to do something about this? Surely the Mission School should teach these Wular Lake folk how to avoid such happenings in future. You fellows must swim across this lake, and show them that it is possible to save their lives by swimming." The teacher said this was impossible. So I said we should have to make the impossible possible.

With this determination in our minds, we set to work when we returned to Srinagar to tackle the impossible. We made it a rule that every boy in the schools should have passed the swimming test of 70 yards by the age of thirteen, otherwise his father would have to pay extra fees. Many parents objected to this rule. My answer was: "Take your son away and put him in a school where they like non-swimming gentlemen." We won through and some hundreds of boys passed the swimming test every year.

At last, the day arrived when I thought the attempt to swim across the dreaded Wular Lake might be made. So, on a beautiful September morning in 1906, we arrived at the lake, having travelled the thirty miles down the river from Srinagar in our dhoonga. At 7 a.m, the swimmers dived into the lake for the five-mile swim to the farther shore, three Brahman teachers, one Mohammedan and myself, Dr. Sam Barton accompanied us in a boat in case any of the swimmers should need medical attendance.

The first half-mile of the swim was a trifle dangerous owing to the weeds. After that, the water was deep and clear until we reached the single beach at a village nestling under a pretty twin-peaked hill. On the top of one of the peaks is a tomb sacred to a Mohammedan saint named Baba Shukr-U-Din, to whom the boatmen are accustomed to give money to secure a safe passage across the dreaded lake. It was a very pleasant swim except for the sun, which gave me a sore back for a day or two. Three of the swimmers found the swim too much for them, and climbed into the boat following us; but Darim Chand and I reached the village beach. The dreaded Wular Lake had been swum. The impossible had been made possible.

Honour Boards

In the school hall, are the honours boards, not as in our public schools in England, proclaiming only scholars and athletes, but for body, mind and soul.

Board No. 1 : For pluck, skill and endurance. Those who have swum five miles across the Wular Lake or the eight miles across the Dal Lake and down the river to the school: or have leaped from the roof of the school, fifty feet up, into the river.

Board No. 2 : The top boy in the school with the most marks for body, mind and soul.

Board No. 3 : Those who have risked their lives for others. The pluckiest deed each year, chosen from the various instances of life saving in the year. In one year thirty lives were saved by members of the C.M.S schools.

Board No. 4 : The kindest deed to an animal.

Board No. 5 : Those who have given their lives for others and on that board hangs the beautiful picture of Jesus Christ, "The Light of the World", who has shown us the way.

Roll of Honour

A roll of honour normally gives details of the achievements of students both in the field of scholarship and in the field of sports. But in this case, we are recording for posterity, names of some of those sacrificing individuals who as teachers dedicated their lives to produce, train and educate boys who would be MEN. We wish we had the names of all those wonderful teachers who served.

Following are the names of some of Biscoe soldiers but, we are sorry we do not have names of many more stalwarts who served in the Mission Schools.

Shankar Koul
Sridhar Bhat
Nand Lal Bakaya
Samsar Chand Kaul
Ishar Kaul (Ishi Kakh)
Chander Pandit
Shambu Nath Kachru
Niranjan Nath Fotehdar
Shyam Lal
Janki Nath
Sham Lal
Dina Nath Matto
Prithvi Nath Razdan
Shambu Nath Matoo
Govind Kaw
Tikka Lal
Kanth Kaul
Govind Razdan
Bala Koul
Dwarki Nath

7

Pandits and the Durbar

WHILE the plains Kashmiri Pandits were making rapid headway towards excellence in services in British India and other princely states, those left behind in the Valley had a late start. The first Pandit graduate came out of Delhi College in the mid forties of the ninteenth century. In comparison, the first batch of graduates from S.P. College, Srinagar, came out in 1911.

However, with the advantage of knowledge of English, many Pandits both graduates and non-graduates were able to get employment in the various departments of Jammu and Kashmir Government. Hardly anybody from 1911-1931 held the post of the head of a department. This was because the State Government wanted experienced officers from British India. The other reason was that admittedly very few Pandits were qualified for such jobs.

The areas in which Pandits made efforts and succeeded were education; both school and college, law; both bench and the bar, civil services and a few in medicine and engineering.

Prime Ministers of Kashmir

In 1846, Pandit Tilak Chand Munshi was P.M. at that time when Maharaja Gulab Singh reached Kashmir after the Treaty of Amritsar by which he became the ruler of Kashmir. Munshi was perhaps the last Prime Minister of the Sikh rule which lasted just over two decades.

The first Prime Minister of the composite State of Jammu and Kashmir was Dewan Jwala Sahai. He was given this as a reward by Gulab Singh. He belonged to Emanabad. It was at that time reported that it was Sahai who arranged the money which Gulab Singh paid to the British and thus in gratitude, Gulab Singh made him Prime Minister in "perpetuation in his family." This meant that Sahai's descendants in the male line would become Prime Minister after his death.

This seems to have happened after Ranbir Singh became the ruler. His Prime Minister was Dewan Kripa Ram who was the son of Jwala Sahai. Following are some of the prominent Prime Ministers of Kashmir.

Year	:	Name
1912	:	Dewan Amar Nath.
1927-28	:	Sir. Albion Bannerji, ICS
1931-32	:	Hari Kishen Kaul
1932-37	:	L.t.Col.EJD.Colvin
1937-43	:	Gopalaswamy N. Iyengar
1945-47	:	Ramchandra Kak
1947, Sep.	:	Janak Singh
1947, June-Oct	:	Mehar Chand Mahajan
1947, October	:	Sheikh Abdullah

In the police, the senior most officer was Pandit Prem Nath Dhar who in the late forties had become DIG. So far, in the history of Jammu and Kashmir only one Pandit became the IGP (DGP), that was Pandit D.N. Kaul who later on took over as the Director General of the Border Security Force (BSF). The peculiar thing about police service was that very few Pandits volunteered for it. And in the forties you could count on the finger tips the number of Pandit Sub-Inspectors in the Police. In the fifties, a few others like M/s. G.N. Kotru,

Manmohan Wazir, J.N. Hashia, Ashok Bhan, Kabu and others were the few gazetted officers.

The only area in which we seem to have attained some degree of prominence and excellence was medicine. Dr. Gasha Lal Kaul on his return from England was appointed Director of Medical Services. And a few others like his younger brother Dr. Girdhari Lal Kaul, Dr. S.K. Shangloo, Dr. S.N. Peshin were some of the prominent doctors in the community.

In private practice, the greatest pioneer was Dr. Omkar Nath Thusu. He lost his wife in a tragic accident when the car in which they were travelling caught fire and she could not be saved. In her memory, he set up the Rattan Rani Hospital which is even today running and serving the people of Srinagar.

In the field of law, perhaps greatest and the first was Pandit Justice Jia Lal Kilam who was lawyer par excellence, a writer and a social reformer as also a leader. There were others like Justice M.L. Bhat, Justice Ashok Bhan. District and Session Judge Neelakanth Hak was the Judge who sentenced the Maqbool Butt to death for murder of an Indian diplomat in Manchester. Unfortunately after the militancy began he was one of the first to be murdered.

In the field of engineering, the first person that one can remember is A.N. Thusu, Chief Engineer and P.N. Wanchoo who retired as Chief Engineer, P.W.D. He was holding this post during the tenure of Bakshi Ghulam Mohammed when the construction and road building activity was at its peak. The other person that one can recall is Radhakishen Pandit who was also a Senior Engineer. There were many others after them especially, those who were recruited in the fifties and sixties. In our own neighbourhood (Narpirastan) we had the two Darbari brothers, Moti Lal and Hreday Nath.

In the field of social service, Kashyap Bandhu leads the way. His famous poem asking the womenfolk of the community to shed the pheran and the Taranga and replace it by the dhoti/saree was a hit in its day. He was also instrumental in bringing about social reform such as widow marriage. Apart from that, he was a great selfless leader and great journalist who gave a boost to the fledgling Martand and introduced an innovative idea called "Mochphal" for fund raising for this social programmes. It is unfortunate that those in power did not understand his worth nor did many of his contemporaries within the community.

Another brave soul was Gopi Krishna who also advocated and agitated for widow marriage and social reform and one could in the fifties and sixties hear their names discussed in connection with any activity at Sheetalnath (Head quarters of Kashmiri Pandits' Voice). There was respect for them from our elders (they stuck their necks out) and awe from youngsters like me.

Others who were prominent were Pandit G.R. Kabu, Pandit Shyam Lal Saraf (who was National Conference Minister for a long time) Dr. S.N. Peshin, Janki Nath Sapru, Janki Nath Zutshi, Pandit Prem Nath Bazaz who were also prominent in the political and social areas of life. In the mid forties Pandits were culturally quite alive, according to Justice Jia Lal Kilam, in his book *"History of Kashmiri Pandits."*

8

Limb of Law

Lawther Shahi

IN July 1931, there were communal riots in Kashmir. Maharaja Hari Singh had ascended the gaddi in 1925. So, only after six years of ruling the state, he faced the most severe test to his rule. He was an extremely progressive ruler to whom history has been very unkind.

The twenties were a period, when modernization of administration had started making great strides in the valley. This was the next stage to build up from the valuable contribution made by British missionaries both education-wise and public healthwise. No one can forget the Neve brothers and Biscoe Sahib. He gave the community the tools with which to face the modern age; along with him were Hadow and earlier to him was Sir. Auriel Stein, the famous explorer. In the second and third decade, we had Sir Peter Clutterbuck who was the Chief Conservator of Forest. Maharaja Hari Singh inherited the state from his uncle Pratap Singh. He had to move carefully keeping in view the problems faced by Pratap Singh who had to undergo severe persecution by the British who needed it as a pretext to annexe the state to British India.

It is well known that in 1931, the small feudatories of Poonch, Mirpur, Rajauri and Riasi were already getting ready to revolt, egged on by the Punjab Muslim League directly and the British indirectly. It was at this point that Hari Singh's mother went to Lahore and met Raja Hari Krishen Kaul and requested him to come to Kashmir as Prime Minister and restore order and save her son. Hari Kishen Kaul agreed and arrived in Jammu from Sialkot along with a very capable police officer Jeevan Lal Muttoo who became his personal aide.

Until 1931, the Police in the state was headed by nominated people chosen by the palace/durbar. It was Hari Kishen Kaul who insisted on bringing an officer of his choice to handle the insurrection. The man whom he chose was B.C.A. Lawther who belonged to the Indian Police, NWFP cadre He was a unique officer who believed in having proper appreciation of the natives. He hated the imperial haughtiness of the British Officer who took the White Man's burden too seriously. His work in NWFP was superb and mainly dealt with intelligence and he retired as DIG, CID of the province. He could speak Urdu and Pushtu fluently like a native.

On sensitive assignments, he would dress like a Pathan with a suitable haircut and would easily mingle with the natives to pursue his investigation. He was responsible for rescuing the wife of a British Deputy Commissioner of Peshawar district who had been kidnapped by hostile tribesmen. By a strange quirk of fate, Lawther was at this time on leave in England. It was extremely embarrassing to the British Government to have the wife of the district chief kidnapped in the district itself. After many discussions, it was felt that only an officer who had earlier dealt with tribesmen could rescue her. At that time travel between India and UK was only by ship, but fortunately for the British Government, the Imperial Airways had started an England-Australia service via Karachi. A telegram was sent to Lawther to return immediately. He was ordered to come by the Imperial Airways flight to Karachi which he did, the only luggage he had with him was a holdall, his dog and his crate of whisky.

The story ended happily as Lawther on returning to Peshawar donned his Pathan dress and ventured deep into the tribal territory where he located the kidnapped lady, paid a ransom for her and brought her back home.

In June 1931, Lawther retired from service as DIG and was packing his bags to go back to England. It was at this time that Hari Kishen Kaul invited him to become the IGP of Kashmir State, which he accepted. Lawther was a no nonsense man, who was not afraid of anyone in the British establishment. He had contempt for the ordinary British Officer and would refer to Col. E.J.D. Colvin who later became the Prime Minister of Kashmir as "Son of a tongawala."

It was the combination of Kaul and Lawther aided by Muttoo that helped to put the insurrection down. Lawther was a bachelor, the only relative he had was an elder sister who tried and tried to get him to marry.

After he took over as IGP, he re-organized the department and got rid of many corrupt and inefficient officers. At that time apart from the IGP, the State of Jammu and Kashmir had only three DIGs, one for Kashmir, one for Jammu and one for the CID.

Within three months, he had pinpointed two DIGs who were thoroughly corrupt. His daily routine was such that nobody could predict where he would go for inspection. Within the first few days, after taking over when curfew was in force in Srinagar, his department needed money urgently for expenses. No banks were open and the State Treasury had been locked up with all the officials running away. He strode with his staff to the gate of the treasury, had it opened and went inside himself, took out rupees one lakh. When the frightened official, who had been summoned from home, timidly asked Lawther as to how he should describe the withdrawal in the Treasury records, Lawther replied "Write, Bahukme, Lawther Shahi" by the royal order of Lawther. It was translated into English and this piece of paper is still in the archives of the Jammu and Kashmir state. He had only one relaxation — he would sit at home with a glass of whisky in his hand, his dog near his foot and his orderly in attendance.

Lawther belonged to the British working class, his family had worked in India for generations and he had a great sympathy for the lowest strata of society. One day he had a conversation with his orderly, which revealed this.

> Sher Afghan, how many constables have I dismissed?
> "None Sir" came the reply of the loyal orderly.
> How many DIGs have I dismissed?
> "Two Sir"

Lawther wanted the approval of the small man with whom he sympathized. After conditions had returned to normal in 1931, he fell into the routine of going for lunch and despite the fact he had an official driver (Pandit Shyamlal, one of the few Kashmiri Pandits who took to driving a vehicle), he would drive himself. He had a fabulous car, a 1921 Mercedes Benz convertible which had once belonged to King Ammanullah Khan of Afghanistan.

During this period when Indian revolutionaries like Madan Lal and other contemporaries of Bhagat Singh had started using guns and bombs, Lawther had been put on what the British had called "Anti-terrorist operation." He arrested Madan Lal who was a comrade of Bhagat Singh. After that, the terrorists had targeted him and one of the reasons for getting a convertible was that he could see in all directions, which was not possible in a closed car.

He was feared as a very strict officer, but it was known that he was fair and just. One day, he left for lunch without his driver and on reaching Lal Chowk (in these days it was called Amira Kadal Chowk and later Palladium Chowk and finally after 1947 Lal Chowk) in Srinagar, he found the traffic constable who should have been on duty at the traffic island, missing. In those days, the number of cars on that road were few and the IGP's car with the magic number JKP-1 was known to all. With a screech the car braked to a halt in the middle of the road. He parked on the side and came out, climbed the steps and started directing the traffic in the place of the constable.

The unfortunate constable was across the road smoking a cigarette. The cigarette fell from his hand and he knew that not only would his job go, he might even be jailed for dereliction of duty. The pawnshop wala looked at him and he looked at the IGP standing directing traffic. With a sigh of resignation, he loosened his belt and crossed the road and stood in front of Lawther at attention and held out his belt to the IGP.

Lawther understood and since the entire Chowk population was watching, he stepped down and in his best parade ground voice told him to put his belt on and get back to his duty. He got into his car and drove away. Within minutes everybody in town came to know about it.

Many people at that time were curious to know how an Englishman had agreed to serve under an Indian and that too a Kashmiri Pandit.

The story goes back to the time when Lawther had just become a DIG and the incident of the kidnapping of the DC's wife had taken place. After the lady was restored to her husband, the Governor of the province felt that the respect of this officer had been irretrievably damaged. Hence, he was immediately transferred to a district in UP. Now the question of a replacement arose. The kidnapping incident had emboldened the hostile tribesmen who were making boasts in the bazaar that they would kidnap the wife of the next officer also who came to Peshawar.

A great deal of soul searching within the establishment took place. It was felt that even if an unsuccessful attempt was made on the wife of the new Deputy Commissioner, it would be bad for the morale. Hence a search was launched for a result oriented successful Indian officer to replace the Englishman and take over as DC Peshawar. The man who was selected was Raja Hari Kishen Kaul who years later became the Prime Minister of Jammu and Kashmir. When rumours started that a retired Indian Commissioner from Punjab was coming and that too a turbaned Brahmin from Kashmir, the tribals enjoyed a good laugh. Where the British had failed, how could the Indian succeed?

Hari Kishen Kaul is part of the tribal folklore. He was strict, ruled with an iron hand and the crime rate practically fell to zero. It was a part of Lawther's duty to meet the Deputy Commissioner for maintaining law and order in the district. And that's how Hari Kishen Kaul and Lawther knew each other.

> Speaking of Kaul, Lawther declared that:
>
> I am not afraid of the Viceroy or the Governor, but I am afraid of that man. You know he can get my pension stopped.
>
> And thus ends the Lawther Shahi period in the history of Kashmir. After he left, all the IGPs of Kashmir till 1947 were British.

After Law and Order had been restored, summer gave way to autumn and already there was a nip in the air and one fine day it was the last week of October 1931 — time for the Durbar move when the Government moved from the Srinagar to Jammu. While certain offices of the Police Department moved to Jammu, the IGP was the last to go. His famous convertible Mercedes Benz was going to cross the Banihall to Jammu and he had with him his driver and his PA. It was a very powerful car with a left wheel drive and Lawther chose to drive himself. His driver who accompanied him sat in the back seat along with P.A Sapru.

It was intensely cold as they started to climb the Pir Panjal Mountain. The winding road was negotiated with ease by Lawther. Soon it began to snow. The two passengers at the back were shivering but they dared not ask Lawther to pull down the hood. Now snow began to accumulate on the front and the back seat of the car.

The only defence that Sapru had against the intense biting, freezing cold was his packet of cigarettes, an expensive brand called Gold Flake. He kept on chain smoking to keep out the cold and thankfully he had enough stock. Eventually, the next day they reached Jammu.

Several days later, once the office started functioning in the first week of November at Jammu, Lawther called Sapru to his room and after discussing certain official matters with him casually asked.

> How many children have you got?.
>
> Sapru was totally surprised at this question and blurted out, "One, Sir".
>
> Can you afford Gold Flake Cigarettes on your salary

Total Silence. Suddenly Sapru realized that during the car drive, Lawther had been watching him through the side rear view mirror of the car and therefore knew during the journey he had smoked the entire packet of cigarettes.

That evening was the last day when he smoked a cigarette. He gave up smoking when he was 28 yrs old and did not touch a cigarette until he passed away at the ripe old age of 90 years

Whisky Hospitality.

When the 1931 riots broke out they were largely engineered from Punjab by the pre-partition Muslim League. Small Rajas and Chiefs of Principalities like Poonch Rajauri and Mirpur revolted and a great many killings took place before Raja Hari Krishen Kaul and B.C.A Lawther were called in to control the situation and put down violence. Overall, there was not that much of violence in the valley itself as there was in these places especially in Mirpur and a small place there called Samnani.

Since this area in the Jammu province was the bigger trouble spot and there was danger of it spreading to Jammu District, Lawther took the decision to go there and control the situation. The Prime Minister ordered a unit of Dogra Cavalry to accompany the I.G.P. Law and order had broken, down and on the way Lawther's party saw the results of the handiwork of the anti social elements.

Men had been murdered, women kidnapped and houses burnt to the ground. Most Government officials had run away. The police was totally conspicuous by their absence. On arrival at Mirpur, he found out that those who were responsible for the violence were still in town and pretending to be on the side of the forces of Law and Order.

Calling his assistant, Lawther ordered messages to be sent to these petty Chieftains to come and meet him. Chairs were spread out under a huge tree and they arrived in a delegation, were asked to sit and explain their version of the recent events in Mirpur. As expected, they lied and lied and lied. As each one was explaining his fanciful position, Lawther was getting impatient and angrier by the minute.

Earlier, to show his friendship and hospitality, he offered from his private stock, which he carried with him, whisky to the petty Chieftains. With each one lying, he soon reached a stage where he decided to take matters in hand. According to the plan prepared earlier, he signaled the commander of the cavalry unit to surround the group and ordered his immediate staff to handcuff them.

The guests were shocked as they were led away by the police. The whole place emptied as evening was falling and Lawther's classic comment was, "The damned fellows, they drink my whisky and yet they tell me lies".

A minute later he shouted "Sher Afghan, Humara whisky le ao." By this time, his Alsatian dog sauntered out and

Lawther was at peace with the world although the nearest part to him was in flames.

By August/September when peace had been restored in the valley, calm and quiet prevailed in Srinagar and autumn came and soon it was time for the Durbar to Jammu. It was during British rule and Christmas was an important festival for the British Officer. As usual, Lawther had purchased about 200 Christmas cards, which in those days had to be hand written and signed with individual messages. Even the outside cover of the card had to be written by hand.

As usual, part of this work was done in the office and Lawther handed over these 200 Christmas cards to a clerk in his department where my father was also working. The clerk in question took custody of the cards and promised to go the Post office and find out how much stamp each one should have, buy the stamps, paste them and post them.

Just ten days before Christmas, Lawther asked my father whether the clerk in question had posted the Christmas cards. My father asked the person concerned and found out from his nervous behaviour that something was wrong. Eventually, he got it out of him that he had lost all the 200 Christmas cards and was afraid to face the IG, BCA Lawther. But he had no alternative except to confess to his crime. A first, the singsong type of English that the clerk spoke did not make any sense to Lawther, but when he understood he hit the roof. He started screaming and shouting at the clerk and threatened him with dire consequences, but being a balanced person he understood what had happened and nothing he would do could bring his Christmas cards back. He took my father aside, gave him money told him to buy fresh cards and sent him away from the room.

Now the clerk was standing like a condemned wretch in front of the IGP. Lawther looked around trying to think of some punishment for the clerk. But he could not think of anything that would punish him but spare his family. In sheer frustration, he looked around the room and saw a Remington typewriter in the corner and suddenly an idea came to him.

"Go pick up that typewriter." The clerk was mystified but rushed forward to obey. "Now put it on your head." In the thirties of the twentieth century, Kashmiri Pandit clerks and others all wore turbans. Thus the typewriter gently rested on the turban perched on top of the clerk's head. It was a ludicrous sight for my father to see when he returned from the market with fresh Christmas cards that the guilty clerk had already begun his punishment. On enquiry he found, that Lawther had ordered the clerk to go up and down the length of the room with the typewriter on his head one hundred times. This was his punishment.

After about half an hour, Lawther called Sapru and told him in a very quiet subdued, controlled voice.

"Go and tell him to stop." By this time the clerk had only done 20 laps across the room.

So much for Lawther Shahi.

Lawther, B.C.A was awarded C.I.E on June 3, 1931.

Heroic Cop

The Dal Lake perhaps is as famous as the name of Kashmir itself. It was during the time of Maharaja Pratap Singh that Srinagar got its first paved roads. As was the normal practice, the first automobile to come to the Kashmir Valley and owned by one living in the valley was the Rolls Royce of the Maharaja.

As in every other city in British India, the princely states also emulated them. The cantonment area began to make its appearance in almost all the princely states and Kashmir got its share of it. The only difference was that in the beginning, it was called the Civil Lines area beginning with Residency Road, Dal Gate and the adjoining road to the lake itself which was given the high sounding name "Boulevard." Of course, the cantonment had already made its presence felt in the early twenties and was known as "Badami Bagh."

These areas were more or less out of bounds for the local population. Only the British and other European visitors would be seen motoring down the Boulevard or taking an evening stroll on the road adjoining the lake.

Our story begins at the time of dusk during the early autumn when there is a nip in the air announcing the arrival of winter. A well-dressed English gentleman, obviously an official of the State Government accompanied by his Mem Sahib, was walking on the footpath near the bend where the road in the shade of the Shankaracharya Hill bends to the right.

There is a small hollow in the hillock where in 1920, a police outpost was set up for security because there had been reports of thefts in the area.

In this police outpost, there was a constable who was keen and enthuastic about his work. He took the warning given by the Sub-inspector about thieves very seriously. In a house, a little away form the police outpost, a thief was trying to escape because the owner on seeing him raised a hue and cry.

Our heroic policemen heard it and reacted with speed and efficiency. He gave chase and was steadily gaining on the thief. Unfortunately, he came out of the lane and started running on the footpath where the English couples were strolling. The thief passed them and so did the constable in hot pursuit. Just at the bend, the constable caught the thief and was grappling with him.

By this time, the shadows had come and darkness had fallen. The Englishman officer saw two natives fighting and decided to take action. After all they had disturbed his evening walk.

He strode forward and shouted, "What is going on here." Both the constable and the thief were busy trying to subdue each other and did not hear his voice. The sahib was now furious and decided to take a hand in the matter. Leaving his wife a few feet away, he strode forward and aimed a strong kick with his boot on one of them. Unknown to him, the kick fell on the constable and he turned round and when he saw an English Sahib, he immediately stood up and saluted him and explained that he was a policeman chasing a thief.

Mollified a bit, the Englishman said "Carry on," but in the meanwhile, the thief seeing that the attention of the limb of law was diverted momentarily, ran away and now the poor constable stood helplessly, while the Englishman wanted to know why he had let go of the thief when he turned round to talk to him.

Within minutes, everyone in Srinagar knew about it. All that can be said in the defence of the constable was that he was in awe of the white man. He was terrified after he saw that the thief had fled. Just goes to show what people thought of the All Mighty British even in a princely state.

P.S: This constable it may be noted was promoted later and retired honourably as Sub-Inspector.

Hari Singh Ka Raj Hai

It was late October almost 10 years after Maharaja Hari Singh ascended the gaddi of Jammu and Kashmir state. Hectic preparations were on for the Durbar move to Jammu in the first week of November. On the spur of the moment, the Maharaja decided to drive to Jammu. The decision was taken at 4 p.m. and just two cars started off from Srinagar towards Qazigund en-route to Banihall.

Prior to this, there had been reported a number of cases where wild animals had come down to the road and attacked travelers in buses, cars and trucks. So the Government, under instruction from the Maharaja, had passed an order that between sunset and sunrise, no vehicular traffic would be permitted on the Banihall Cart Road (B.C. Road).

But such a rule would not be applicable to the Maharaja and his retinue. By the time, he would reach Qazigund,it would be dark. The IG was informed and promptly messages were flashed all along the route. The Maharaja was accompanied by only his driver and his pilot car (open car) Dinshaw Patel was the pilot.

Now the Maharaja had a strange fascination for speed. The pilot car was a Chevrolet and the Maharaja's car was a Rolls Royce.

The two cars were proceeding smoothly when the Maharaja asked his driver to speed up and overtake the pilot car, which was leading the way. As the Maharaja's car crept closer to the pilot car, the pilot desperately urged his driver to go faster, but the Rolls Royce overtook him. The pilot kept on shouting at his driver to go faster. Fortunately, they were driving on a straight flat road between Khanabal and Qazigund. The driver of the pilot car became increasingly nervous as the VVIP car had overtaken them and was almost a mile ahead.

The driver did not notice a small depression on the road and the convertible that he was driving went over it with a thud. The pilot sitting in the back seat was thrown out and landed in a nearby ditch. The driver did not even know that pilot was no longer in the car. He kept on driving and was relieved to see in the distance that the Maharaja's car had stopped. The Maharaja came out and was laughing. The driver turned around to talk to the pilot, but found the back seat empty. Nervously, he looked back and saw Patel running towards the car. Huffing and puffing with exertion Patel ran towards the Maharaja saluted and profusely apologized. The Maharaja enquired whether he had been hurt. Patel looked at his king and said:

"No, Sarkar. Only my dignity is hurt. I should have been ahead of you," Patel said looking at his mud-splattered uniform.

"Let us proceed further," said Hari Singh. So off they went at a much-reduced speed. By this time, it was nearing 6 O'clock and darkness had almost set. Both the cars had their headlights on and the beam of the Rolls Royce headlights could stretch for more than a mile. As the shadows increased and it became fully dark, the pilot car suddenly slowed down when the driver saw about a 100 sheep under the control of a shepherd (Bakrawal). The sheep bawled out and began to run helter skelter. The Bakrawal was shouting and trying to control his flock.

Meanwhile, the two cars slowly reached close enough to the milling sheep and the Bakrawal. The driver shouted and Patel shouted more, but to no avail. Finally, the Maharaja's driver also joined in the shouting. The Bakrawal was getting increasingly frustrated and angry.

> The following conversation ensued.
>
> Hurry up and push your sheep out of the way. Do you know who are delaying, you stupid Bewaquf?

"What do you mean? I have as much right as you have on this road. Do you know, this is Hari Singh's Raj and I will complain to him and get justice from him," the Bakrawal shouted back.

In the Rolls Royce, the Maharaja heard the dialogue, smiled to himself and got out of the car. The headlights lighted his face and the Bakrawal's face was a study in shock. He went down on his knees and stuttered "Sarkar." Hari Singh ordered him to get up and told him to take his time in collecting the sheep and crossing the road. The Bakrawal rushed to do his bidding with the two drivers, the king and his pilot watching the scene.

The episode closed with the Maharaja presenting Rs.100 to the Bakrawal (This was a princely sum in those days)

And so, the Maharaja went to Qazigund, the sheep went across the road and the Bakrawal could not believe his good fortune.

Peel

E.G.B. Peel, who succeeded Lawther as the IGP, was considered a misfit in the Police force because he held a Master's degree in Literature from the Oxford University and was proud of his scholarship. He joined the Indian Police and served for most of his career in UP. He was a DIG when he was offered the IGP's post in Kashmir. He had a violent temper and since he had served in U.P he knew all the profane curses in Urdu. As UP was known for its culture and polite language he would sometimes flare up in anger and shout at someone in front of him, obscenities ending in a euphemistic the "ji" at the end was perhaps a concession to the culture of U.P. His wife used to say that it was his temper that came in the way of his promotion to the IG rank in UP. She was as sober as he was temperamental.

When Peel came to Kashmir he brought an official P.A. with him. In those days P.A. to the IGP was a gazetted rank and generally an ASP or an SP would fill the post. The man who came along with Peel was W.H. Archbold, a handsome man, a bachelor and an efficient police officer. Both of them, Peel and Archbold, having served in British India, had enough experience of internal and external intrigues. Since Archbold was younger and single, he was out practically every night dancing and partying. He was the most sought after dance partner at the Residency dances.

An interesting incident concerns him. He had a Alsatian dog. In the evenings, Archbold used to change into civilian clothes and leave his service revolver in the drawer in his bedroom.

There was at that time a Sub-Inspector who wanted desperately to become an Inspector. He thought of a plan. He arranged for one of the domestic staff of Archbold to go into his bedroom and steal his service revolver. The deed was done on a night when Archbold was out dancing and the only occupant of the house was his Alsatian. The next morning, the theft was discovered and Archbold was mortally afraid of his boss Peel's anger. He kicked the poor dog taking out his anger on him with the words "what the hell were you doing when the thief came."

After a while, better sense prevailed and the IGP's Office Superintendent who heard about the theft, made discreet enquiries, told Archbold that it was an inside job because the dog would have certainly barked if the thief was a stranger. Well, the revolver was found by the man who had arranged the theft without Archbold knowing about his scheme. With the revolver back, the Sub-Inspector was transferred to police lines.

After several years in Kashmir Peel left Kashmir and Archbold succeeded him as the IGP in 1939. Peel went to Mysore and stayed there till 1943, when he finally retired.

Peel's wife was a very sweet natured motherly type of woman. Once she and her husband were driving from Khanabal to Srinagar when they stopped at the roadside to cool the engine of the brand new Morris car which Peel had purchased recently. The car being new, the hand brake when applied would give out a screeching sound. The driver Sham Lal was always afraid whenever he had to apply the brake because Peel Sahib would invariably shout obscenities at him, ending "ji" in his vintage style and say, "are you trying to ruin my new car."

The driver used to be petrified since it was the IGP shouting at him and one day he turned up at our house and fell at my father's feet begging him to save him from the wrath of the Sahib. So one day, choosing the right moment, he told Peel "Sir, please don't shout at Sham Lal. In a new car, this always happens." This was the 1936 Morris model just then imported into India.

At Khanabal, a small incident took place when their pet dog wandered from the car and a curious villager looked at it. The dog barked, the villager got scared, picked up a stone and threw it at the dog. It got hurt and ran back to Mrs. Peel who was sitting in the car. Instead of saying anything to the villager for having thrown a stone at the dog, Mrs. Peel shouted at her own dog and said the following immortal words. "Why did you bark at him. Serves you right."

It has been stressed earlier in this narrative that Peel was very proud of his penmanship especially in the English language. After coming to India, he also studied Urdu and could speak, write and read the language like a native.

One day, as usual, he had dictated a certain memorandum in which he had used a slightly lesser known word, which my father could not understand. However he took it down as Peel spelt it out for him and after he left the room, consulted the Oxford English Dictionary, where he discovered that Peel had given him the wrong spelling.

As soon as the typed memorandum was placed before him, he began to read with his pen in his hand. He came to the offending word and began to shout:

> I gave you the spelling of the word and you still make a mistake, you put in the wrong spelling.
>
> But Sir that was the wrong spelling.
>
> Are you trying to teach me English?
>
> No Sir, but the Oxford Dictionary says so.
>
> I don't believe it, let me see it.

The dictionary was brought and it was seen and proved conclusively that the Oxford educated English Inspector General of Police of Jammu and Kashmir State was wrong and the humble Kashmiri Pandit clerk was right.

"His face was a curious mixture of puzzlement and confusion," said Mahadeo Sapru years later while recalling this incident.

Peel looked up at his assistant and said these famous last words.

"I have been damned all my life. I thought these were the spellings, but they are not. THANK YOU SAPRU FOR CORRECTING ME. I AM GRATEFUL."

When Peel's term of office came to an end, he was invited by the Maharaja of Mysore to become the IGP of Mysore, which eventually he became and finally retired in 1943.

But when his term was ending, the Kashmir government was looking for a successor to him. And in Princely States, seniority was not strictly adhered to as in British India. Most requests from Indian States for posting a British Officer to them were processed by the Political Department in New Delhi and it was suggested that since an British Officer was already in Kashmir, he could be offered the post of IGP and could succeed Peel. The Political Department was referring of course to Archbold who was a senior SP.

Bell, Ronald. S

By the time RS Bell took over as IGP in the mid forties, Mahadeo Sapru had throughly stablized himself in his position as a key person in the IGP's Office. He was also promoted as the Office Superintendent of the CID and would advise the Police Chief about the politics of the department as also the integrity and efficiency of the officers.

One such case comes to mind where he tried his best to mete out justice to a poor humble constable who was victimized by a high ranking officer who was a DIG. This officer had suspended the constable who hailed from the Jammu region and prior to this had forcibly transferred him to Kashmir Province. When he put in a representation, he was told by someone close to the DIG, that he would have to pay a certain sum if he wanted his suspension revoked and he transferred back to Jammu Province.

On a constable's pay, he could not meet the demand and was forced to sell his wife's gold jewellery after which he paid the money. Despite this, the suspension continued and since in those days there way no subsistence allowance during the period of suspension, he had come practically to starvation level.

He knocked at many doors, but nobody could buck the DIG. At last, some one suggested to him that he should approach the right hand man of the IGP who they assured him was totally honest. So one day, this half starved constable appeared at our house and requested to see Mahadeo Sapru who already knew about this case.

Looking at the man in this pitiable condition, Sapru decided to do something about it. Bell, his boss, was a very reasonable and even-tempered man. So a few days later, he approached Bell after lunch when he was in a good, expansive mood and related the entire background of the case to him.

> Since it comes within the DIG's powers, I don't think I can do anything about it, said Bell.
>
> But Sir, you are the Chief of the Police Force and the lower ranks look upon you as their God and father. Justice demands that something should be done to put this man out of his misery. After all, the Police Force has more constables in it than DIGs
>
> For a few minute there was pin drop silence and then Bell looked up and said
>
> Do you have a solution?

Yes Sir. You have overriding powers under the Police Act and you can overrule anyone's decision. If you approve, we can from the Central Office issue an order reinstating the constable and cancelling the suspension period by treating him as on duty for it. Apart from it, we can also issue a transfer order transferring him back to Jammu. That way he will have some money with which to live on and will be able to go back to where he came from.

All right, do it.

Within minutes, the two orders were ready and signed but not released. A trusted subordinate was sent to search for the constable who was sent under escort to the Accountant General's office to identify him so that he could draw his TA and his back pay. Without an order in writing, he would not get anything.

So, Sapru went personally to the AG's Office and handed over the order to Pandit Premanand who was then the Accountant General of the State. The money was delivered to the constable and he was not allowed to roam around lest he be identified and the DIG informed about his reinstatement. At night, he was accommodated in a trusted person's house and early next morning, he was sent in a goods truck to Jammu and told to report to a Police Officer there to whom Sapru had already given detailed instructions.

For the constable, it seemed like a dream. That he was grateful was expected but his greatest fear was that he would be caught before he was out of the reach of the DIG. But he managed it and when Bell asked Sapru about it, he said that Justice had been done.

Many years later in 1965 when this writer and his father Mahadeo Sapru were at the Tourist Reception Centre trying to book a seat to Pathankot, a man suddenly came from behind and saluted my father, who just stared at the man. By this time, my father had long since left the Police Department and asked the man as to he was.

"Sir, I am the same constable whose life you saved during Bell Sahib's time."

Suddenly, the light dawned and my father smiled and asked him, "So how are you, where are you posted now?"

"Sir, I am now SP, Ladakh. Sir is there anything I can to do for you now. Have you come to buy a ticket?"

"No thank you, we just bought a ticket."

And that is where it ended, but one does remember an Englishman's sense of justice and an Indian's determination to see that it is done.

9

Family Saga

Towards Excellence with Austerity

LAKSHMAN Joo Sapru was a valley Kashmiri Pandit. Not much is known about him. He had two sons whose names were Baghwan Das Sapru and Sridhar Joo Sapru. Baghwan Das Sapru had two sons Raghu Nath Sapru and Mahadeo Sapru. Sridhar Sapru had four sons and two daughters Our story concerns Baghawan Das Sapru's two sons. Unfortunately, Bagawan Das Sapru died in his twenties leaving behind a widow Sonamal with two children and no means of support.

It is a miracle how she survived and brought up her two sons, educated them, got them married, saw her sons building a new house and had the pleasure of playing with eight grand children of whom my cousin sister (Kanta) is the youngest among the girls and yours truly is the youngest among the boys.

She was a determined woman who fought doggedly against all odds. Though she was illiterate, her fund of commonsense would put to shame any statesman or diplomat. Being a widow, Grandfathers cousin did not look on her with favour but while keeping all the customary behavior pattern going, she saw to it that her two young ones would be taken care of and survive to grow into manhood.

In this, she was greatly helped by her elder son who had inherited most of her sterling qualities. Raghu Nath Sapru had a one point programme in his life since he was acutely conscious of the poverty of the family and that was to achieve excellence at all costs and as far as possible not be too much of a burden on his poor widowed mother. He was a student of the state high school to which he used to walk every morning. He had no time piece at home to know the time when he should leave home for school.

One day, he was late for school and was admonished by the teacher. He was in a dilemma. How to tell the teacher that he did not have a timepiece. But he was a great innovator and had loads of commonsense. He went home and woke up the next morning bright and early and watched the sun's rays falling on the wall of the house. He brought a piece of chalk and marked it because the suns rays had reached that particular spot on the wall at exactly 8 clock and that would give him a guide for reaching school on time.

Unfortunately, though the new system worked well, he did not take into consideration the change in seasons when the sun's rays would fall at a different place at the same time. However, he managed it eventually. He was a brilliant student and even before his matriculation, he was a scholarship student and right through he was an extremely hardworking student. He had no interest in games or sports but was waiting impatiently to get into a profession.

Soon, he completed his high school and again won his scholarship to go to the engineering school where they trained Civil Engineers. It was not a an Engineering College as we think of today, but where the nuts and bolts of the profession were adequately taught leaving improvement and advancement to the ability of the individual student.

Contrary to what is being propagated today about the Dogra rulers of Kashmir, they were in fact extremely progressive and brought modern education to the valley along with the new *lingua franca*, the English language. It was during Maharaja Ranbir Singh's reign that the need was felt for having trained staff to man civil engineering projects and irrigation works. For this, the Maharaja started a polytechnic, which was appropriately named Ranbir Polytechnic. It was here that he got trained and passed out with flying colours as a scholarship student. In later years, people would point to him and say that "Without crossing the Banihall, he became an engineer."

In those days, the initial appointment was as a Sub Overseer. This was the initial job given to train people who did not have a degree from an Engineering College, but were otherwise adequately tecnically trained. The next post was Overseer. Today, this corresponds to what is called a Junior Engineer.

The day he passed out, Grandma (we grand children called her Kakni) heaved a sigh of relief. She was sure now that her son would soon be employed. From our grand-mother's side we were related to the family of Raja Hari Krishen Kaul and with a qualified candidate it was easy to put in a word and get the job.

Raghu Nath Sapru was a dedicated man who took life very seriously as all the children in the joint family realized. He had no use for entertainment and leisure activities. He was a true karmayogi who did his duty sincerely towards his family including half-baked products like his and his brother's children.

After his appointment, his mother made plans to get him married and selected a girl from the Kaul (Bagh) family of Rainawari. She was Raj Rani Sapru and she presided over the joint family for many years after her marriage. Meanwhile, her mother-in-law had one more hurdle to cross and that was her younger son who was a total contrast to his elder brother.

Mahadeo Sapru was a peculiar combination of the middle class and an ambitious young man who wanted to get ahead in life. However, he was susceptible to distractions like any other young man of his generation could be. He had a colourful personality and would easily impress people by his command of the language, both Urdu and English. He had a taste in fine arts such as Music, Poetry and even games. He played hockey, broke his arm once and was, in short an exuberant young man.

Once when he was studying for his second year in college he made a spelling mistake in an essay, which was otherwise excellent. The lecturer to express his extreme annoyance gave him zero out of ten and that incensed this student of FA (in those days the first two years of college were called FA for Arts and FSc for Science). He soon made up his mind that continuing his education was no good and would not help him. He decided to qualify himself as an engineer and set about searching for a subject and an institution.

Money was, of course, a problem but by then his elder brother was the confirmed bread winner of the family and the family decided that he should go to Calcutta to study Wireless Engineering. This was in 1929. Prior to this in 1926 after he finished his FA he was married to Padmavati Kaul of Ali Kadal, daughter of Pandit Raghu Nath Kaul, a retired Customs official.

On arrival in Calcutta, he discovered the unpleasant fact that he had no interest in Wireless Engineering and promptly switched to learning shorthand and typing which was a short duration course compared to Engineering and returned home in time to witness the 1931 riots in the Kashmir Valley. At that time, he was given an opportunity of service and was employed in the Prime Minister's office for a while and subsequently in the Police Department, which he served till 1947.

Many years later, when he was enjoying his retirement, he once told me about how disciplined and strict Kakni Sonamal (Grandma) was towards him, her younger son although in her heart of hearts she had a soft corner for him.

As explained earlier, by temperament Mahadeo Sapru was an individual with fine tastes and interested in music, drama, arts, games and other finer things of life.

Once there was a music performance in Srinagar that we call "Gyaivun" and I had gone to see this performance. Mind you, I was already married by this time and could be considered a full fledged adult. I had mentally promised myself to go home by 9.00 p.m but soon forgot the promise and finally woke up when the performance was over at 10.30 p.m. In those days, there were very few street lights though I knew my way. I finally reached home at 10.45 p.m.

At that time, my brother was posted at Handwara and there was no other male member in the house. As soon I knocked the door, I expected my wife to open the door. It was my mother who did and as soon as I stepped in the house, she slapped me hard on the cheek. I was shocked beyond words but what she said was still worse.

"If something happens to you, who will go out to look for you? Do you expect me to do that." And with that, she marched to her room and I was left, a highly chastened man who had learnt his lesson the hard way.

The two brothers were a contrast in temperament and taste and the eight children in the joint family instinctively were afraid of "Babatathu," the elder and would prefer to approach "Toth," the younger. In summer, quite often Uncle used to get up early in the morning and bang at all the doors waking everybody up with the words.

"Get Going And Do Your Morning Ablutions."

Very often my father in whose room I used to sleep would shake me awake with the words "Get up Quick Babatatha is calling you."

As we children grew up and were able to discuss and mildly criticize some of the sayings of our parents, the one thing that has remained over the years in our minds is that "He would talk about what Chief Engineer Khan said, this and that and he would talk about what Peel Sahib and Bell Sahib said" On rare occasions, when everybody would sit together for the evening meal the two would talk and we children would simply be seen and not heard.

All through our childhood, the children were made conscious of the fact that the Sapru family name was famous and noble and we were expected to live up to the standards of our forefathers. In this connection, very often we heard a name — Sir Tej Bahadur Sapru and we had a vague idea that we were somehow related to him. Whether we are or not, the fact remains that a Sapru anywhere in the world shares the same Gotra with every other Sapru.

Years later, when I was an experienced field correspondent, many in Delhi would ask me whether I was related to the Saprus of Allahabad. My answer would be "No, but we are country cousins."

Discipline at Home

Learning to tell the truth is a part of any child's education. What he or she learns at home becomes his equipment to face the rigours of life.

Two small events come to my mind. After I recovered from an illness, my father purchased a bottle of horlicks out of which I would get one spoon mixed with milk every morning. After a few days my brain began to scheme as to how I could reach the sweet powder and eat it. The tin was placed on top of a high cupboard, which with my three feet height I could not reach. But being resourceful, I dragged the stool and managed to grab the tin and swallow the few spoons of powdered horlicks before putting it back.

I thought I was safe. But next morning I was caught. I knew that I was going to get a beating but surprisingly my father suddenly gave me an option, "Tell the truth, admit your mistake and then I will not beat you." I did it and escaped the beating but in the process learnt a lesson for a life.

On another occasion, my father had purchased a thermometer, which was at that time a rarity in our home. It was always opened by him, used for any member of the family who was sick and put back. I was always curious about it and wanted desperately to handle it. The opportunity came and I did it, but fear of discovery made me nervous and I took the thermometer in my hand to the bathroom where it slipped out of my nervous fingers and broke. I was in jitters, put the broken thermometer into its case and put it back and waited for the punishment. Here too justice was merciful and I escaped punishment and remembered the earlier occasion. Needless to say, these were my only forays into petty crime and lying.

Life in Winter Snow and Sleet

Life in winter in the Kashmir Valley was indeed difficult and misery was the watchword.

The three parts of winter namely Chellay Kalaan, Chellay Khord and Chellay Bache together formed the most severe period of the rigours of winter. Today, most housewives even in the Kashmir valley would be horrified if they were to be asked to do without cooking gas, kerosene stove, heaters and pressure cookers. But women in those days had to bear the brunt of shortages which were treated as something which one had to live with.

One has to remember that the concept of the *bukhari* (it is a big metal pot in which wood or coal is burnt and it generates heat for the entire room) was not prevalent or known in the Kashmir valley. One could see bukharis only in Government offices and other prominent places. The only means of heating was and is the *Kangri*. This is a native fool proof method of personal comfort.

A *Kangri* is by definition a mobile personal heater for a person. It has a cane handle and the outer body is made of cane to ensure that the user did not burn his hand. The inside portion is an earthern bowl in which usually coal is burnt and it produces enough heat to keep the man in less discomfort. Often, one can see on the roads people wearing long loose gowns called *pheran* with a slight bulge which signified that he is carrying a Kangri under the cover of his *pheran.*

In the last hundred years, the climate has changed very much in the valley. Earlier, the winter used to be very severe. Very often, six feet of snow would fall not only in the village but also in the city of Srinagar. The snow would block the door of the house and the fear of being locked up inside kept people awake at night. In fact, for many years one member of the family would remain awake and keep a spade handy so that if too much of snow fell, he would shovel and clear the path from the door to the lane or the road.

The worst part of living in such conditions was that the housewives had to, in freezing cold, fetch water from the tap sometimes quite near and sometimes far from the house. Those living near the rivers and the streams would also have to trudge in mud, sleet and very often over ice to fetch *a not* (a traditional round shaped pot for water). It was worse for Pandit women in villages.

Once the snow starts falling, it is easy to walk on it. Once it stops snowing, the snow on the ground gets hard and turns into ice and God help you if you are careless in walking over it. It has no shape, it has all kinds of shapes and which is the best and the easiest way to get a broken ankle. Added to this problem is that of movement through lanes and by lanes where the traffic is less unlike on the road where constant march of feet would flatten the road, and make things easier for the pedestrian.

The next danger was from Shisharghant (icicles). They are of two types. One where snow forms into ice and due to forces of gravity perhaps points from the edge of the roof towards the ground. In fact, it is shaped with a broad base and keeps narrowing as it comes down. There was always danger of it falling on an unsuspecting person walking on the road or in the lane or under the roof of the house. There is another type of Shisharghant which develops in the opposite direction and the narrow point is pointed upwards. These are usually found in caves and mainly outside cities. Scientifically speaking, the one that points from up to down is called *Stalagcites* and the one that points from bottom to top is called *Stalagmites*

When Grandma Passed Away

"She was my grandma and her name was Sonamal but we children called her Kakni."

The winter of 1951 was really severe and we were enjoying our winter vacation. In the rest of India, the longest vacation that the students enjoy is the summer vacation, but in Kashmir students need the longer vacation in winter.

Grandma was sick and fortunately her elder son, my uncle, was in Srinagar but her younger son, my father was away in Amritsar working as Food Procurement Officer of the Jammu and Kashmir Government in Punjab. Grandma was under the treatment of a good doctor but even we children could sense that her end was near.

The doctor came at 6.00 p.m. it was already dark. He examined her, gave her medicine and left without a word. She went into a coma and started addressing her elder son as her younger son. Disjointed words pointed to the fact that she wanted both her children by her side but it was not to be.

She died at midnight and by morning a telegram had been sent to my father. But try as he might he could not come since the road route was blocked by snow and there was no air service due to bad weather. He wired back that he could not come.

Many years later he told me how he felt at the death of the only parent he knew and had. "The only thing I could do was to fast for the day but carry on working. I calculated when the 10th day would be and the thirteenth day would come and on those days would go the temple. This I did."

But to get back to the morning of the funeral Myself and my cousin both 11 years of age were given the task of informing our relatives about Grandma's death. The farthest point we had to go to was on one side Ali Kadal and on the other side Sathu Bar Bar Shah and Rainawari. We too had to go with our clogs and wearing our pherans, we started out on to the lane, which led to the main road.

Between our house and the main road a distance of about 300 yards we slipped on the ice at least three four times and once the Kangri which both of us carried practically overturned on our thighs and would have burnt us had we not been quick enough to get up.

On and on we went to reach our destination, delivered the message and were back at home in three hours. Just goes to show you how difficult transport was in those days and without two legs one could never survive especially in the hellish winter of Kashmir.

Strangers to Luxury

While radio was admittedly a luxury which made its appearance in Srinagar in limited quantities around the year 1946, luxuries in our locality were few and far between. The only sample of modern technology in our house was this cycle which in those days was not only considered a luxury and an asset to have, but it was also not called cycle. It was called "BICYCLE" and on a rough estimate of over seventy five thousand Pandits in Srinagar hardly 15 or 20 had this new method of locomotion.

As a child grows beyond ten years of age, especially a boy, galloping towards teenage, he starts dressing himself and generally becomes conscious of his appearance. In those days, barbers used to go to the houses of the rich. But the poor had to sit in his open shop on the ground for him to cut their hair. At that time, the current fashion was to cut the hair all-round short with a little bit left longer in the front. We called it "Bichur" and every boy of that age would insist on having a hair cut of that nature.

I remember crying my eyes out when I was not given the Bichur haircut while my elder Hreday got it. But after the deed was done, nothing could be done, but I resented it for a long time.

As we grew older, we became conscious of a new thing called filim and a new place called talkie. The name has come from when cinema made its apperance all over the world. The original name was Bioscope. Later on, it continued since it was only visual. And later on that period was called the silent films era. When sound was added to the visual, the place of exhibition was called talkie because one could hear sounds. Subsequently, it was named cinema.

The first cinema in Srinagar was the Palladium Talkies. In fact, the word talkies were written along with its name for a long time on its frontage. Among the younger generation the word cinema was whispered because in our value system then, going to the cinema was an evil thing to do. We heard elders discussing among themselves Mr. X whose son was seen going into or coming out of Palladium Talkies.

As time passed, gradually attitudes changed and we used to discuss new filims without having seen them. If one of our friends saw it, the whole group would know the story line and by then radio had started becoming fairly common. In the early 50s Radio Ceylon's commercial service broadcast songs from latest Hindi films. Thus, we would hear the songs either from the neighbours house or from the paan shop on the road which would be blaring out the songs especially at the time when we would be returning from the school.

In the absence of pocket money, many of the boys would skimp, beg, borrow and steal coins and when they reached the magic figure of seven and a half annas which was the lowest ticket available to enter the Palladium Talkies, he would be in the seventh heaven. Those who managed to collect the money, would always go for the 3.30 show because they had to be home before dark. However in our family, there was no question of going to cinema as there was no money. We only listened to other boys with our mouth open as they recounted the adventure of getting the ticket, going into the darkened hall and sitting on wooden benches and guarding your seat so that some Hanji boy (boat man's son) who were sturdy and stronger than Pandit boys, would not occupy the bench seat.

Apart from this, one instance will illustrate the security phobia of the Pandit. Earlier it was mentioned about how my mother as a bride had to wear a burqa to hide her face when coming for the first time to her husband's house. As late as 1946, physical security of the women folk was a primary concern for the family. And growing up girls were not allowed go out of the house. They had to be protected at all costs.

Once we were playing and this must have been in our psyche. Hreday, Jagan, myself were playing. Our youngest sister, who must have been barely three or four years old, insisted on playing with us. We were playing our own version of cops and robbers. And we had a big bed sheet over our heads and we were trying to protect our house against attack.

But overriding factor seemed to have been to protect Kanta first the youngest baby sister. And the cry was "Hey, we should hide Kantinath." The Nath attached to her name by us was to bring it in line with our three names which all had the word Nath as our middle names.

The only piece of luxury that I can remember from my childhood is a gramaphone with a manual charger. I was told that when my father had purchased it, none of us children were allowed to touch it. It was a great novelty and all the eight children except the eldest daughter who was by then already married, would have our mouths open looking at this marvel which produced beautiful music and songs.

In the early and middle twentieth century, a wall clock had become a normal fixture in middle class homes but, we were more or less strangers to the wall clock. It was only when my uncle bought an alarm clock to wake us up early and get ready in time for school, that we became familiar with the time proclaiming itself from the shelf on the wall where it was perched. When uncle bought his first wrist watch and the first one in the family, I stared at it and wanted desperately to touch it.

Reverting to the cycle and its impact on our life, it was the sole conveyance of the family. It must be said here that until the late seventies, most people in Srinagar walked. After all, most distances either to the school or to the office or to the hospital or the main market were on an average not more than five kilometers away. Only the few affluent could afford to move around in tongas. All five of us children learnt how to ride a cycle on that good old British made Hercules. Being the two youngest ones, I and my cousin Jagan used to sneak out of the back garden gate along with cycle on Sundays when this two wheeler had a holiday. In front of our house, two hundred yard away was a newly laid road appropriately named Nai Sarak. On this road, I must have fallen at least more than a dozen times. But the amazing part of that is that I never suffered an injury which would be visible at home for which I would receive a beating. On one occasion, I fell into the big open drain which even today is opposite to the Kotru and Pandit houses located there and hopefully now also on the Nai Sarak.

On the subject of my family, I have referred earlier in this narrative to my father and my uncle. They were two brothers each with his distinct personality perhaps influenced by their respective but totally different jobs.

While the elder one was very serious in his approach to work and life, one suspects through great many hardships and privations in his effort to come up, the younger one was playful, and tended to be at times mischievous. He played football and hockey and in one altercation with a member of the opposite team broke his left arm.

When he was in college, he got the urge to play badminton. This was around the year 1920-21 and to prove it we have an old photograph which he must have taken in the first commercial studio in Srinagar. Pandit Vishwanath of the company of the same name was in fact the pioneer of commercial photography in the Kashmir Valley. He was a student of the Mission School and greatly influenced by Biscoe Sahib. Years later, my father's interest moved to music and for a period of nearly 10 years he played the sitar, which he carried with him to Amirtsar when he was posted as Assistant Trade Agent of the Jammu and Kashmir Government in Punjab.

One can only sum up. While poverty is our constant companion, it has its moments of glory when ordinary things become sought after luxuries. So much for luxuries in the midst of poverty, the shining light in the midst of darkness.

Take Him with You

The first boy in the joint family went out of Kashmir for studies to Lucknow. The entire clan watched him leave and wished him luck. On this day, on a cold cloudy November morning, he was going to Jammu *en route* to Lucknow and as his luggage came out, from across the other house came the voice of a humorous elder.

Take X with you. He has not seen the world.

Right. I shall take him with me. After a short pause.

No, I don't think so. The weather is cloudy and it will be very cold there

Of course. Geography did not enter into it. He did not have the foggiest idea of the difference in weather, temperature between Srinagar and Lucknow.

But then it was a dialogue that they had gone through many a time and would go through many a time more.

From the twenties onwards one can say that the modern age began for the Pandits. A great many ideas and information from the rest of India and the world began to filter into the valley at fairly frequent regular intervals. For instance, the arrival of the radio and the telephone. While the telephone was a distant luxury confined only to top officials and very rich people, the radio did not seem so unavailable.

Snake Charmer

Yet, not many could dream of possessing a radio. In our mohalla of Narpirastan, there was only one family which had a radio set. The set was in the room of Professor Nand Lal Darbari a legendary Professor of Chemistry who must have taught thousands of students the mysteries of this science. He was a very popular gentleman lovable, generous to a fault and as most professors are prone to be absent-minded. Once, he was walking towards his college, to deliver his lecture at 3.00 P.M. *en route* at Chrinkal Mohalla as he reached the slightly wide space in the road (remember in those days every body including Professors had to walk) he saw a crowd collected around what turned out to be a snake charmer.

The long and the short of the story is that he totally forgot the class and became completely absorbed in the antics of the snake and of its master.

Radio Dialogue

On the day Mahatma Gandhi was assassinated in 1948, the news was broadcast by All India Radio and most adults in the neighbourhood of the Darbari clan house went to the good professor's room to hear the details. We, kids, did not understand except that Mahatma Gandhi had been killed. We trailed behind the adults and stood in the doorway as the sober, somber voice of Melville Demello came over the Radio announcing that the funeral of the Mahatma would take place the next day and that AIR would broadcast a running commentary.

As the radio went silent our Professor suddenly shouted at it "Kar?" What he meant was at what time the next day which the announcer had not given. There was pindrop silence, some giggles and a few snickers.

For years after this incident, people would say "Kar?" and smile at each other.

Angrees Ball (British Ball)

Vilayati Hoon (English Dog)

For the children of that age and generation entertainment was mostly self made. Most of them belonged to families where it was always a hand to mouth existence. Yet, appearanaces had to be maintained. Clothes might be old but they had to be washed and pressed even though many holes would have been repaired diligently by the housewife. Quite often, food was kept overnight, since it was precious and eating the previous day's food the next day was quite common. One of the most common was "Bathe Thi Kaenz."

Normal expenses left very little spare cash for buying either toys or sports items for the children. Cinema was in its infancy all over India and Kashmir. In fact, the valley got its first cinema in Srinagar in the thirties. It was the Palladium and for a long time this was the only cinema in the entire city.

Subsequently, it was joined by the next one Regal and immediately there after independence by Amrish. While Palladium was located just on the Lal Chowk where it is still is but in a ramshackle condition.,practically ready for demolition.The other two namely Regal and Amrish are located on the Residency Road and the place is also known as the Regal Chowk.

Social values were such that going to the cinema was considered to be a crime and any one seen by his relatives or friends coming out of or going into the Palladium Talkies, the news would spread like wild fire and stories would be spun behind the unfortunate person's back. Apart from that, there was the question of money. Pocket money for children which is taken for granted today was unknown. Once a boy, who heard a classmate in school mention the words pocket money and saw the boy spending it on sweets, hesitantly raised the subject at home was given a tongue lashing. "Bathe Yed Chai Phatan" (Your belly gets filled up).

The obsession was centered around studies. For the children, especially boys, the game plan was to do well, aim for the best and manage with what he could get. For the girls, till as late as the fifties, education was a luxury and many of the older sisters in the family remained illterate while the younger ones were lucky enough to get the benefit of education. Thus, the moment the father came back from work, if he saw the son idling away, he would get annoyed with him and in most cases give him a beating. So, there was hardly any time or opportunity to play.

One of our cousins was the only child of his parents and he had purchased for him a ball. This he naturally brought down into the Aangan and all the children wanted to play with it. While we were playing with it, we made sure that it did not go over the wall into our neighbour's house, which was at a slightly lower level. As the heat of the game intensified, one of us kicked the ball and we watched with our hearts in our mouths as the ball curved gracefully and was about to fall into the neighbour's garden. At the last minute, due to some freak alteration of one of Newton's Laws of Motion, the ball did not fall on the other side but on our "branda" (porch) We heaved a sigh of relief and that brought forth famous last words on the subject.

This is an Angreez ball. That is why it did not fall on the other side. It is a special ball my father has bought me.

The same boy pestered his father for a dog. His father was posted at a police station in Rainawari. He tried to divert the boy's mind, but the child was adamant. So after the futile effort to dissuade the boy, he asked one of his constables to get a stray dog, tie a rope around his neck and pretend that it had been purchased from the market.

When the boy saw the dog, he was happy and the dog was put in a boat and brought home, *en route,* the canine felt like having a bath and the constable accompanying the boy allowed it to jump out of the boat and swim along the boat for sometime. The boy was thrilled that he had a dog who could swim while he himself could not. The father sitting back in his office was worried sick because he knew that his wife would not tolerate a dog in the house.

Eventually, the dog and its young master reached home and he lost no time in announcing it to us children in the Sapru compound. And the piece de resistance of his declaration was "It is an Angreez Hoon. You know he can swim" Poor boy, he did not know that all dogs can swim.

Having pets was unknown. Only the rich and the famous could do that and even there within the seven bridges there was hardly anybody among the Pandits who had a pet dog. This idea was brought forth by a few Kashmiris whose ancestors had migrated during Aurangzeb's rule to other parts of India and whose descendants had distinguished themselves in Civil Service and been employed by His Highness Government. Animals were not taken into the house and leather was totally taboo. Shoes had to be left outside and gradually a passage was designated for leaving the shoes.

Our generation which grew up in the forties of the twentieth century played "guli danda" which was obviously imported from Punjab. In our local dialect, it was called "Lathkinj Loth." Usually the big stick bat (danda) and the small "guliu" were made by carpenters as they were finishing any work for our parents and we would beg them to make. Usually, they obliged.

"Kaisi Achi Hai" (How nice she is)

It was Mission School at Anantnag and the two brothers were studying there. Their father was posted at Khanabal in the PWD.

The younger one was a boy of poetic nature with a fine sense of appreciation of the beautiful things of life and he had been watching for days together a little girl who was practically of the same age as he perhaps was, in the single digit phase.

One day, he was standing in the school ground as a bunch of girls including the object of his admiration passed by. He couldnot restrain himself and said these famous last words: "Kaisi Achi Hai"

This was heard by someone who carried the tale and spread the news. It became big news and reached the teacher who immediately ordered the culprit to be produced before him for punishment and advised others to beware.

Similarly as often happens there are all kinds of catty comments about teachers behind their backs. In this case, the children had also made up a profane couplet which they kept on chanting before the teacher came.

"This plus this is Jagirkakin. . . ."

While chanting it in a class with the teacher absent, it was just nice amusement and our artistic hero's elder brother also in his enthusiasm started chanting this chant.

The leader of the choir was a mischief-maker and stood directly in line with the door to the classroom. He could see the teacher coming and promptly sat down while the others, including the hero's elder brother did not notice and were caught red handed while shouting the profane poem.

Of course he was punished, while the instigator escaped.

Homely Homilies

He came home tired from Handawara. It was a tiring bus journey and he was hungry. As he got down from the Tonga on the main road near the Narishori shrine at Narpirastan, the shop keeper across the street shouted for some one to carry his luggage to his house. Part of the luggage carried beautiful juicy corncob known in Kashmiri as Makaiyi Wut.

This was a periodic ritual for him to bring these things for the children. As he entered, he called to his youngest and asked him as to where everybody in the family was. This youngster was playing with his brother and did not think it fit to reply. Eventually another question was asked:

"Suin Kiya Chuve Ronumut?" (What is the vegetable that you have cooked today?)

He did not known the answer, but his brother whispered "Wanus Nyuk Nyuk Zuin" (Little pieces of wood). The prompting was faithfully repeated by the boy and the man was angry at the response. Since the word Suin and Zuin rhyme, it was thought to be a very good repartee but it was in poor taste for a man tired and hungry, the bread winner of the family to hear from his children. And the poor boy had to suffer his anger.

Very soon the mother arrived and peace was restored and after a good meal everybody went to bed. The next morning, restored to his good humour, the man went about his business and in the afternoon decided to take his young son for an interesting outing.

Just at the time when the boy was supposed to accompany him, the father could not find him. Looking all over the place, he finally traced him to the toilet. Patiently, he waited and once the boy was ready father and son went out together.

On the way, the father smothering his annoyance, explained the paradox of time and place, opportune and inopportune to his young son thus:

"Once upon a time there lived a hunter. One day, he was searching for prey. Whole day he searched he could not find anything. He was getting hungry and his dog accompanying him was also feeling listless. Just as dusk was falling and he had given up getting any animal to fall to his bow and arrow, he saw a deer in the distance.

Instantly, he whistled for his dog but there were not response and by the time the dog trotted upto his master, the deer had vanished and the hunter was angry. The dog had let him down at the right time.

Out of this has come the proverb, "Kute nu shikar vale hagnu aya" (At the time of the hunt the dog was otherwise occupied with. . . .)

That is the moral of this story.

A Ruse to Save the Logs

What do you do, when you know that without help you cannot save your property and will surely lose it. All the hard earned money going down the Vitasta. And that is precisely what nearly happened many years ago to these two brothers Raghu Nath and Mahadeo Sapru. After both the brothers had got married and had jobs, their mother felt they needed a bigger house and for that land was first to be purchased.

In front of our old ancestral house, was the land of our cousins who had built their house at Safa Kadal. Though physically they had shifted from Narpirastan, their land was still next door to us and it made sense for us to buy it from them. They were also two brothers Pandit Arjun Nath Sapru and Pandit Radha Krishen Sapru. After the usual negotiations, the land was brought and gradually building materials was acquired and construction started in the late thirties and continued into early forties.

Our story takes us to the time when my uncle purchased wood for the woodwork to be done for making doors and windows in the house. For this massive logs purchased in Baramulla were floated down the Jhelum to be taken out at Razdan Yarbal.

On the day the logs arrived at Razdan yarbal, the boatmen tied them together with ropes and left for their homes. Unfortunately, the river was in spate and the pressure of water broke the tightly knit grouping of logs. A man came running to the house and Mahadeo Sapru rushed to the river bank and began shouting at the top of his voice:

Razdan Sahib's logs are being washed away. Somebody come and help Somebody come and help

Hearing the name of the celebrity of the locality, all the boatmen who were sitting and eating the dinner in their dhoongas, came rushing and within minutes the logs were securely tied.

The crisis over, the ruse worked and the logs were saved. But next morning the boatmen found out who the real owners of the logs were.

The Romance of Durbar Move

It was during the rule of Maharaja Pratap Singh that the Durbar Move became a regular Government activity and not just an annual move by the ruler of the State to escape the cold harsh winter of the Kashmir Valley for six months.

Geographically, Kashmir valley is in the middle of a range of the Himalayas and Jammu is in the plains.After, it became one entity, a state in 1846, the Jammu and Kashmir state, it was necessary to pay equal attention to both regions. Durbar move, was a device to keep people of both regions happy.

Practically half of the Pandits employed in the various departments of the State Government used to move in November from Srinagar to Jammu and the Secretariat would function from there, leaving a skeleton administrative staff in Srinagar. Because of the valley being snow bound during six months of the winter, hardly any activity took place there. So practically every Pandit family had one member at least going to Jammu for the winter and the refrain among the housewives was that the "Durbar Move is coming and we are going to Jammu."

It was a romantic adventure, a change and a new experience for the housewives. They would meet different people and pick up a few words of Dogri and Punjabi. They would also get a chance to study the eating habits of the people of Jammu and I suspect that the first Pandit valley housewife who saw a chapathi must have seen it and tasted it in Jammu along with Dal both of which were practically unknown as the staple food was rice and hak in the valley. However, the number of wives going to Jammu was very small.

For the children, it was a series of daily doses of excitement just to get ready for the Durbar Move which in the early days was a two and half day journey by a bus over nearly two hundred miles of a road hewn out of the sides of a mountain in the Pir Panjal range.

A word about transport. After 1892, when the arch at the highest point on the Pir Panjal was built by a British Engineer and mistakenly called the Banihall Tunnel, roads began to be laid down to cater to the needs of people using that newly developed magic vehicle called the automobile. Initially,the only automobiles seen were those either owned by the Maharaja or by the few Englishmen serving in his Government or a visitor coming in from British India especially the province of Punjab.

Emulating other princely states like Mysore, Travancore, Hyderabad, Baroda, the Kashmir Maharaja also ordered the laying of roads especially on the trunk routes over which horses and tongas used to ply. By the early twenties, an urgent need was felt to have a regular transport service during summer months from Srinagar to Jammu and other important towns of the state.

There was at that time all over India a gradual expansion of modern transport and a new business was developing in terms of providing point-to-point bus service over fairly long distances. Initially, as in civil aviation, so in surface transport, the first move towards commercialization was carrying of mails from point to point. In the case of Kashmir, it was Messrs N.D. Radhakrishan & Company that were the first mail carriers and pioneered transport in the valley. They carried mail to various points in British India like Rawalpindi and later on Jammu. The first one was on the Jhelum valley route which was an all weather road that was cut off in 1947. The other route across the Banihall was usually open for six months.

Initially, the only access to the rest of India from the Kashmir Valley was through the Jhelum Valley Road (J.V. Road), where the last point to cross was the Kohala Bridge across the Kishenganga River. From there a road to Rawalpindi was open along with the Rail Link. In the Jammu region, from which Kashmir Valley was cut of during the winter months, a new link was established to the railhead at Sialkot in Punjab. This line was subsequently extended up to Jammu.

Thus the British and the state administration largely depended on these two routes for to and fro movement with British India. One suspects that had the Dogra rulers not held

Jammu, the Banihall Cart Road (B.C. Road) would have remained a dream. While trade and industry utilized the Jhelum Valley Road, there was initially hardly any traffic on the B.C. Road. However even the J.V.Road would get blocked by snow whenever there was heavy snowfall on the Murree Hills.

The B.C. Road now called the Srinagar Jammu National Highway was originally built as a private Cart Road for the Maharaja of Kashmir in 1913 and was completed by 1915. Since it was only meant for and utilized by the Maharaja and his retinue, it would by sheer lack of use fall into disuse. At the urging of his advisers, Maharaja Pratap Singh threw open the road to the public in 1922 and it was only this which encouraged the passenger and goods traffic to expand and use this road.

It was indirectly and directly the result of the Pakistani invasion of Kashmir that spurred the Central and the State Governments to improve, this road widen it, and construct a proper tunnel at the top of the Pir Panjal Mountain, leaving the old arch (mistakenly called tunnel) as a spare standby tunnel for an emergency. The construction of the new tunnel was started 2000 feet below the old arch.

Construction was entrusted to a Swiss Consortium Messrs Karl Kunz and Company, which started its work in 1953 and the tunnel with two lanes for to and fro traffic was inaugurated by the then Vice President of India Dr. S. Radha Krishanan in 1956.

In a short span of 25 years (1922-1947), the traffic rose from a few hundred tongas and other horse-drawn vehicles to 3,000 trucks annually. Today, more than 2,000 vehicles a day in summer and 1,500 a day in winter ply on this road.

During the pre 47 era, the most prominent bus transporters were Messrs Allied Charag Din & Sons who pioneered the Jammu Srinagar bus service. At the time of partition, they decided to migrate to Pakistan and thereafter others came into the fray.

It is reported that it was Sardar Attar Singh who started one of the first passenger bus transport companies. One thing definitely known is that Sardar Attar Singh had been the "Governor of Kashmir Valley." This designation was actually that of the Deputy Commissioner or the Collector, as he was known in British India then.

So Sardar Attar Singh and Sons started the Bus Service and later on another company by the name Amjit Limited was also floated. In the forties, another company called the Suraj Bus Service was also in operation. Subsequently another private company floated on or about 1947 called the Kashmir Tourist Bus Service Ltd., Simultaneously, after Independence, the State Government also started a Bus Service.

One more family business belonging to the Nandas (today associated with the Escorts Group) also started a service in the fifties to and from Jammu & Kashmir, which was, knows as "Nanda Bus Service." Prior to that, Haji Charag Din & Sons operated their bus services for both passenger and freight in the state connecting Jammu with Srinagar and other places like Anant Nag, Phalgam, Baramulla, Sopore etc.

Most of the buses were twenty to twenty-five seaters and powered by Bedford Engines. Most of the pioneer drivers were Sikhs and to tell the truth it was not just a journey but an adventure when anything could happen.

In practically every family, there would be two brothers a married sister and the children. One brother and his wife and children would move to Jammu leaving the other brother and his family and grandparents in Kashmir. It was among the children that envy and jealousy surfaced because one group was going somewhere nice and interesting, while the other would be left in the miserable cold and "Khatkosh."

And thus came the great day, when on a cold drizzling November morning, I, accompanied by my father walked all the way from Narpirastan to the old Bus stand where our luggage and the womenfolk had already reached courtesy my father's friends. Actually, Shri Gopinath Kadalbijju and his wonderful intelligent and generous wife Danavati used to accompany my mother on such trips. Her husband used to work in the Central office along with my father.

It was a sight to see, to cherish and to remember with that "inward eye which is the bliss of solitude." My father walking wearing winter clothes and with a Police overcoat slung over his arm and me hanging on for dear life to his hand since the traffic on the road was increasingly thick with tongas practically scraping my side. The road was narrow in the forties. It still is.

And so we reached the bus stand. The ladies were seated first. The luggage was loaded. The ropes were tied and the driver arrived. He had obviously been briefed as to who his passenger was. So, more care and consideration. From the Bus stand as the engine note increased, we children were excited at the prospect and looked in wonder at the scenery unfolding. Of course, the children had monopolized the window seats.

Before we could practically settle down, we reached Khanabal and there on the road I saw my uncle. From a distance, I recognized him by his turban and his tall stature. The bus stopped and my father got down from the bus and had a brief chat with his brother. My Uncle "Babatatha" came and hugged me and off we went towards Qazigund. Just before entering the little town, we passed Pampore, Brijabhara and stopped at Qazigund.

Here the driver took the vehicle to the petrol station for filling up petrol. In those days, roughly fourteen gallons were needed to complete the journey to Jammu. It was fascinating for us children to see how petrol was filled into the tank of the bus. Two huge hefty men used to hold the handle sticking out of the pump and move it in a lateral direction to pump the oil into the petrol tank. The reason was that on the highway there was no light available to power the pump electrically.

We reached the base of the Pir Panjal and began our laborious climb on the winding hairpin bends. From a distance, it looked like a number of snakes lying in a circular position with a sheen of snow white on top. At each hairpin bend, the driver would change gears and the engine note would alter into a high pitch as the bus would crawl its way up in second gear.

After a couple of hours of this torture, we children lost interest in the scenery and most of us fell asleep. Soon the bus crawled to a stop and opening our eyes we saw a long line of buses and trucks waiting to cross the tunnel. And that brings us to the profane language used by drivers and cleaners in their wordy duels and dialogues. Often, we heard the bigger boys shout (Turn the handle, zogue, I want to go to the tunnel). This was in the days of the yore when very little of new ideas and practices were imported.

One of the things that tested the mettle of the drivers and the cleaners was the problem of starting the engine in the absence of a self-starter, which came to India many years after it was developed and used in commercial vehicles in the West. The car engine used to be started with the help of the metal handle which when turned with sufficient force would in turn provide the movement for the fan belt to revolve and start the engine. It was for this reason that the majority of the cleaners had to be physically fit and strong to keep turning the starting handle.

We were told that it was a very long tunnel and it would be very dark inside and scary. As we went in, the driver wisely switched on his headlights, which lit the road ahead, the rocks on either side were irregular in shape and to my eyes it looked as if they were devils waiting to catch me. I was frightened but the warmth from my father's proximity helped to reassure me that no monsters would get me at least not in the bus. Finally a long pencil of light pierced the darkness and we knew that we were coming into the bright light, which we did.

Soon we reached Udhampur and from there to Nandini where a shorter tunnel has to be crossed but without any fear of monsters and devils. We were now rolling towards the plains of Jammu and finally reached our destination, safe and sound but tired and hungry.

Geography & Education

On the way to Qazigund, on one of our six monthly journeys between Jammu and Srinagar, I was sitting on the left window seat in the second row from the driver. Childish curiosity and a rumbling stomach made me ask my father as to how far the next station or stop was.

He pointed out of the window and said:

> "Check the milestone" he then leaned over me and pointed to a whitewashed stone on the side of the road on which the number had been written. Father explained that this indicated the number of miles (in those days we had not converted to the metric system), we had travelled since we began our journey from Srinagar.
>
> "We have to travel two hundred miles from Srinagar to Jammu and we have only five miles more to reach Qazigund. There we shall have something nice to eat," he smilingly promised.
>
> Thus it was that I had a practical demonstration of distance calculation and a dose of arithmetic.

Today, what was known for almost a century as the Banihall Cart Road during the Dogra rule, eventually became vital link between Kashmir and the rest of India and Project Beacon of the Border Roads Organization (BRO) of the Army looks after the maintenance of this road which now has the impressive prefix of National Highway.

Life in Jammu

There was a qualitative difference in the life that Pandits led in Srinagar or some other places in the valley and the life that they led in Jammu. By virtue of geography, Jammu being in the plains had more interaction with Punjab than the people of the valley. Also the Dogri language is somewhat similar to Punjabi.

The winds of change that swept over British India, which included Punjab, brought about a certain kind of openness and freedom of movement among the people beginning with the thirties and the forties. Whereas in Srinagar the social interaction between Pandits and Muslims was restricted to a minimum (there was no interdining), in Jammu things were far more free.

Some of the customs and practices followed by the Pandits kept them, in some ways, totally insular. For instance, our eating vessels were totally separate. We drank tea out of copper cups called *"Khos,"* a round shaped cup with a base at the bottom. We also ate on thalis and the cooking pots were also distinct. The only common thing we had with the Muslims of Kashmir was the *Samavar*, which was a pot for making tea self-contained with an in-built stove.

Another important factor was that there were no hotels and restaurants in the old parts of Srinagar in what is called today the down town area of Srinagar. Amira Kadal, the first bridge, was the area which could be considered posh and the Residency Road beginning from Lal Chowk was the area that had fairly expensive restaurants meant to cater to the tourist community, before 47 mostly Europeans and after 47 a mixed crowd of both foreigners as well as Indians who could afford the holiday.

It may however be noted that there were teashops catering to the Muslims. The nearest equivalent to this among the Pandits would be the Halwai shop where one could get milk and milk products as also fried pakoras etc. One important distinction to be kept in mind is that the Muslims used Chinaware for drinking tea especially.

One more distinction has to be clarified and that is the issue of tea and tea drinking. In the Kashmir valley it is even today green tea that is drunk by most people at home. Due to severe winter and some other factors perhaps the tea was never mixed with milk. It was drunk with sugar alone. Today, the five star hotels of India are offering this and it is called, as it has been for centuries in the valley, the ***"Kahwa."***

The peculiar thing about Kahwa is that it was considered to be the poor man's tea and none of the hotels and restaurants on the Residency Road would serve it in their dining rooms. The tea that was served was mainly made of leaves collected and processed by British companies like Brooke Bond and Lipton. In the public mind, this was promptly labelled "Lipton Chai." After independence, within the Valley, the housewives began to store Lipton Tea in addition to the Green Tea.

This is in the nature of an aside to explain the sudden conferment, as it were of freedom to the Pandits in Jammu to visit a Restaurant. Apart from the question of a Hindu Restaurant or a Muslim Restaurant in Jammu, there was a comparative freedom of choice. After the day's work, unlike in Srinagar, most Pandits used to stroll down the road from the Secretariat to the Raghu Nath Bazar and whenever they could afford would go into a teashop and have some *"mathis"* and some tea. Some of the more adventurous ones would go in for butter toast and tea (not available at home). Incidentally, the tea available was only Lipton. Some of the religiously inclined would also go to the Raghu Nath Mandir and pay their obeisance to the god Lord Rama.

Poetic Justice

When making arrangements for going to Jammu at the time of the Durbar Move, every Pandit would have to think of reserving a place in Jammu where he would live either alone or with his family for six months. For those who would be taking their families, it was a more elaborate and difficult assignment. But for those who would not be taking their families, it was easy to join a few colleagues and hire a complete house instead of a few rooms.

In 1946, my father decided to take me with him to Jammu (my mother had died in 1945) and so three other colleagues of various other government departments joined together and decided to hire a cook so that there would be no problem of food. The other three were the usual run of the mill clerks but one of them was a singularly peculiar character.

This gentleman was a Maha Kanjus (terrible miser). As soon as we reached Jammu and the daily routine started, I was admitted to a school and had to get ready in the morning almost at the same time as the four adults. In the very first week, I noticed that this gentleman would wait for another member of the team to go for his bath and would rush to his bed, search under it, take out his small tin of polish and furiously use it to polish his own shoes. For a while it did not occur to me as to why he was doing it until I discovered that he did not own either the polish or the brush, which he could use to polish his own shoes.

There were other small incidents, which pointed to his being a miser. His roommate discovered that his polish was disappearing faster and whenever they went down to Raghu Nath Bazaar he would never pay the bill or offer to pay part of it. The result was that usually one of the other three would have to pay his share also.

There were murmuring about this and I heard the three adults sometime speaking against him. My father counselled patience and said that they would get their opportunity to teach him a lesson. One day, they went to a restaurant and while going, this gentleman swore that he did not have a pie on him, but unknown to the other three, he had a ten rupee note in his top pocket where he usually kept his glasses.

As they sat down and ordered, he expressed a desire to check the menu and ordered something different. The waiter bought the menu and to read it he put his right hand into the pocket to bring out the pair of glasses. As he did so, the ten-rupee note got struck to the arm of the glasses and fell out by the side under the table.

This was noticed by my father and a second person who tried to open his mouth and inform the owner. But my father was too quick and he stamped his foot under the table and said, "What is the matter with you, keep quiet." So the other man kept quiet while my father stretched out his foot and carefully dragged the note towards him, bent down, picked it up folded it into a ball and put it in his pocket.

Now the other three saw it and everyone had a smile on his face. All this while the miser was selecting some choice items to eat for which he knew the others would be paying. At this point suddenly, my father became very generous and displaying unusual hospitality, persuaded the gentleman to order many more dishes.

The long and the short of it was when the entire feast was over and the bill came my father generously took out the ten rupee note and paid the bill which amounted to Rs. 9 and 12 annas. That left four annas, which was given as a tip to the waiter. When he saw the ten-rupee note, he realized that it was his note, but he could not say a word since he had earlier sworn that he had no money with him. A case of poetic justice.

He is a Communist

I was too young to understand what Communism was, but our two eldest brothers already knew enough about Marx,

Lenin, Stalin etc., and there would be discussions which went over the heads of we three younger ones but what brought the subject straight before us was an incident.

Our neighbour whose garden and house faced our front door was Pandit Narain Saraf a former Retired Customs official. It was a beautiful house and we would see the old gentleman daily moving about in his drawing room on the first floor. He had a son named Niranjan Nath Raina. (The difference in the two surnames can be explained as quite a few families even today sport two surnames).For instance, Raina and Razdan are supposed to be similar and there are other instances also of this duality. One day in early November 1946, we suddenly saw police descending on the house and going in for what apparently seemed like a search. After sometime, there was total silence and later on we came to know that it had something to do with the activities of his son Niranjan who was locally known as "Nyari Saraf."

Apparently since communism was banned in the state, the police must have got instructions to arrest him, but he escaped. This happened in 1946 and after independence, he left Kashmir went to UK, did his doctorate in Physics, returned to Kashmir, worked as Professor of Physics in Kashmir University and retired as the Head of the Department and he is now living in Delhi.

But the effect of it on us children was profound. We thought, at least I thought, that Communism was some kind of an infectious disease.

Security Priority

Apart from the normal Muslim rule where each King or Sultan would get toppled by the other, they all had one point programme and that was to convert the entire population of the valley to Islam. In this they were successful. The only period when there was comparative peace and no forcible conversions was that of Sultan Zaina-Ul-Abadin also known as Badshah.

However, the worst period was the seventy years of Afghan rule which commenced in 1753 during which Pandits were physically pushed into gunny bags alive, tied up and thrown into the Dal Lake because they refused to convert to Islam.

It was the darkest period for the Pandit community during which the numbers fell to just eleven families of survivors who hung on to their faith and ethos stubbornly. The only parallel instance that one can think of is the systematic ouster in modern times, is the murder, abduction, and rape of 1989-90. Although peace came during the Dogra rule, the Pandit psyche was never free from fear of physical harm. This was especially so with regard to womenfolk. In the early part of the century, you would hardly find any young girls or women walking on the roads. It was only after the Dogra rule got stabilized that there was law and order to the extent that women could move around safely.

Batta Gajan In the fourteenth century, Zulqadr Khan alias Dulch, a descendent of Changez Khan — his very name, like the sound of a hurricane, fills one with dread, with a force of 70,000 cavalry came from Trukistan and invaded Kashmir. During his depredations, which lasted eight months, he converted the people forcibly to Islam. Thereafter, he left for his native land via Khuri, taking 50,000 Brahmins as slaves. While crossing the Devasar Pass, a snow-storm occurred in which he, together with his own troops and the Brahmin slaves, perished. This place is since called Batta Gajan, meaning the Kashmiri Pandits death-oven. (In Kashmiri, Batta means Kashmiri Pandit).

Even today, the older generation refers to Batta Gajan as one of the worst tragedies to hit the community. Imagine, if those 50,000 Pandits had not perished in that snow storm, today they would have been much more than 5,00,000 and the community would have been one million strong. This expression was used extensively in the 19th and the twenteith centuries to signify any comparable tragedy. It got into the idiom and became a part of the language.

In the twenties, the Pandits had a peculiar custom, which died out immediately after the thirties. Brides when going to their in-laws for the first time in the company of their husbands had to have their faces covered especially if they were coming from an area in Srinagar city, which was suspect with regard to safety of women.

My father who got married in 1926 had a similar experience, which he narrated to me. "We had to go in a barat by boat from Razdan Yarbal and go down the Jhelum to Ali Kadal and go ashore at Rishi Peer waterfront. After the wedding, the same boats carried the bride and the bridegroom but with one variation. The bride though dressed in the current wedding clothing had put on a Burqa.

But why a Burqa? What was the point?

This was a custom from almost one hundred years earlier when there had been cases of brides being kidnapped *en route* to their husband's house.

Security had become such a phobia with Pandits that even a women left alone at home during her husband's absence would ensure by precautions and even guile to convince the bad elements that there was a male member in the house. There was a story of a woman in our Mohalla who used to sit at the window in darkness and put on her husband's turban and smoke the Hookah (Hubble Bubble) to give the impression that a man was in the house.

Football Saga

Actually, it was a short saga. You could even say it was not even a saga, but it did open a Pandora's box of memories that shot out of the brain box after a gap of fifty years. It happened like this.

I (The author), Hreday, and Jagan were desperately in need of a game to play. But we did not have either hockey sticks or a football. Somewhere along the line, (I do not remember how) we managed to get a reject from someone.

Yes, the football was our prized possession and our commander Hreday decided that we should play in the backyard but that was not allowed as my aunt had planted some hakh there. So we went to the front yard, but as soon as he gave it the first kick the football gave its last gasp. All the air hissed out of it and it became as limp as a dead cat.

The football was brought examined thoroughly by three experts and prounced dead. Now arose the question of a reviving it to life. One worthy made the suggestion that since it had a hole in the neck we should go to the cycle repair shops at Malik Aangan. So off we trooped to the cycle shop but disappointment awaited us. He had gone home for lunch.

So from Malik Aangan we went to Razdan Kocha but there the shop was closed and onwards to Bana Mohalla. There too we drew a blank. Finally after Chinkaral Mohalla we found just after Sham Bhat's, a cycle shop with the proprietor sitting idle.

We rushed, we explained, we showed the patient and we requested immediate restoration of the football to good health. He looked at all three of us and did not think we were creditworthy and told us in no uncertain terms that it would cost the grand sum of One Anna to repair the football. We looked at each other and decided to check our treasury. Low and behold, our fortune amounted to three paise (In those days for the information of the uninitiated or the young or the ignorant four paise made one anna)

Shamefacedly, we showed him the extent of our resources and just pleaded with our eyes. This is all we have, please do it. I suppose he felt sorry for us and agreed. We were very happy. We stood around. It was the main road leading to Habba Kadal and we were on the side of the road.

Just then we heard a lady's voice from behind and I saw for the first time in my life a woman on a cycle stopping in front of the cycle repair shop. I stared at her goggleyed and then I discovered that this cycle was different from other cycles. It had no (middle) harizental bar. I whispered to Hreday. He said with the superior smile "Don't be stupid, that is a lady's cycle". My curiosity satisfied, I now watched to see what she wanted.

The cycle repairman had wished her and showed respect and then she was telling him about the problems of the back wheel of the cycle. She suspected that there might be a puncture, which the expert confirmed. So, without as much as by your leave, our work was set aside and the cycle became the priority.

We quietly watched and he sensed that we were impatient but he explained his philosophy. "For this small job of repairing the puncture, I am getting four annas and for your tough job I am getting three paise, see the difference" We meekly nodded our heads and tried to be patient.

Soon, the cycle was ready, the payment was made and the customer departed and our expert resumed work on our patient. Being highly experienced, he eventually fixed the defect and cured the malady after which he filled the football with air and to our delight it gave a very healthy sound of a bounce.

We looked at each other paid the money and did not stop until we reached home. And then we rushed into the yard and started playing but all the gods were against us. The moment the second kick of the ball materialized, it started raining. Frustrated we had to come with our precious ball and sit glumly on the verandah and watch and curse the rain.

But who was that lady, you forgot to ask? She was Ms. Lakhmi (Lakshmi) Rambal one of the first ladies in the valley to take up teaching.

Tiger, Tiger Burning Bright

The road was in an appalling condition. The vibration was shaking the bones of the lone passenger in the bus meant to seat 40 passengers but now completely empty.

It was the sweltering June heat of Punjab, the bus was going from Jammu to Pathankot. The driver was feeling the heat and had parted company with his shirt. The passenger promptly emulated him.

The passenger was the Assistant Trade Agent of the Jammu & Kashmir Government based at Amritsar and recalled to temporary duty at Pathankot. This was just the year after the Pakistani Invasion of Kashmir and there was a terrible foodgrains shortage in the valley. While the State Government did its best to mitigate the sufferings of the people, food relief came from other states and was stacked bag on bag at the railway station waiting to be loaded on trucks for transport to Srinagar.

And that is where the passenger of the bus was going, to Pathankot. Just a few miles after passing the border at Madhopur, the bus was going at a steady 30 KMPH and the passenger was dozing. Suddenly the driver saw lights, twinlights in the distance. All round the countryside it was pitch dark on both sides of the road.

He shook his passenger awake and said:

Panditji, we are in trouble. Those twin lights are the two eyes of a tiger rushing towards us.

Really, then what shall we do? Shall we stop, Shall we turn back.

No Panditji, we shall fight him and we shall kill him.

But with what? Have you got a gun?

No, I don't have a gun but I have this bus.

I guarantee you Sir, that when he comes under the front wheel I shall twist the back wheel so that his neck comes under two tyres at the same time. That will finish him off.

But how can you be sure of going over him. Suppose he turns away and comes at us from the window, his passenger voiced his fears and doubts.

Don't worry, trust me, you will see.

All talk ceased, the driver concentrated on driving. The tiger was coming nearer and nearer with two pinpoints of his eyes lighting up like laser beams. Knowing that he would require every light in the dark, the driver put on his headlights at maximum beam and as they came closer to collision, the driver switched on additional lights, which blinded and dazzled the tiger.

At the first collision, the tiger was thrown back on his side and the front wheel went over his throat. While this was happening the passenger was holding on to the safety rods in front of his seat and the driver was wrestling with the wheel. Suddenly both of them had a crack. The tiger's neck was broken.

After he straightened the bus out on all four wheels and restored the balance of the vehicle, the driver laughed out loud and told his passenger.

Panditji, we have killed us a tiger.

But how can you be sure that tiger is dead. Let us stop and check.

There were about a hundred yards from the dark shape visible even at that distance. They took a few pebbles and threw them at the tiger. There was no reaction. The tiger was dead. Just at that moment, from the opposite side they could hear a tonga, they shouted at the tonga driver to stop and the driver went straight to look at the tiger asked the shocked passengers of the tonga to help him shift the carcass of the tiger from the middle of the road. This was duly done.

The driver reached Pathankot and parked his bus. The passenger took leave of him. End of adventure. End of Story. Not quite.

A year after this incident, the author then a wise young man of nine years was leaving a dhaba in the Shariekhpura locality of Amritsar. As we were leaving, two new customers arrived and one of them wished my father who instantly recognized him as the driver who had killed the tiger. A short conversation followed and we parted company.

"Did he really kill the Tiger?"

"Yes, he did "

"But how? Did he have a gun with him?

"No"

"Were you with him"

"Yes"

"Were you scared?"

"Yes"

Total silence. We walked home and I thought of the tiger and for some reason I sympathized with the tiger. Why, I do not know.

Boot Polish, The Cure All

It was a cold November day and snowflakes were hitting the window panes as I sat with a Kangri under my pheran. It was a gloomy day. I could not play and there was nothing else to do. I hated the books and the homework. I was miserable, in short.

Suddenly, a ray of sunshine came into my life. My uncle barged into the room and told me to arise, awake and get ready to go out with him to the market. I was excited and I fumbled with the buttons of my coat. Finally, we set out and the farthest we went to was Habba Kadal. On the way, the snow changed to sleet. Anyway, my uncle stopped at a shoe shop and announced to me his intention of buying me a new pair of shoes. Oh Boy, was I excited and thrilled. I tried several pairs and found one that fitted me. The usual bargaining began and after an interval of half an hour of intense bargaining the deal was struck, the money was paid and I became suddenly the affluent, proud owner of a new pair of shoes.

I clutched the box to my chest and followed my uncle back home. I didn't show the shoes to anybody, but rushed upstairs to try them on. I put them on and stared at the shining black topside where I could see my reflection in the shine of the leather. I could not go out to try it out, so I walked up and down in the corridor in the front of the room.

After sometime, I decided that I should not dirty the soles anymore and took off the shoes to examine whether I had dirtied them. I had. There were marks of dirt on what had been two shining soles. This was not good. I wanted my shoes to remain as good as new forever, but how to do it. I stared at the sole, I stared at the wall, and I stared at the door. No inspiration.

Finally, I looked into the shoebox where I found a new shoe brush and shoe polish. Idea. I would polish the shoes, I mean, the soles, and so I did and got caught. My uncle caught me polishing the soles of the shoes. My uncle who rarely would laugh especially with us children suddenly burst out laughing.

Sooma, we don't polish soles of shoes. Soles are meant to become dirty. We walk with on them. We polish the top of the shoes. You can't keep your shoes new this way. Now be a good boy and put your shoes into the box.

Close to tears, I was hurt, puzzled and angry at this world. Why can't I keep the shoes new all the time. It's so unfair.

Hey, Sooma, want to see Bansi's new ball. It's an English ball.

I rushed out forgetting all the gloom of a few minutes earlier. Understandable. I was nine years old.

Free Discipline Day

There was excitement in the air and we three talked about it at home. But the eldest among us did not condescend to join our conversation because the next day he, a student of class X, would become a teacher for a day.

So the next day dawned bright and clear, with the boys filling the school ground as usual. Soon after attendance, the "Free Discipline Day" began.

A word aside. This was the Central High School also called Mission School also called CMS School. It was also called Biscoe School. This was the name sometime used by the educated lot but the illiterate lot used to call it "Biscoot Sahib's School." The virtual distortion of his name however did not worry or bother the founder Rev. Canon Biscoe.

He was responsible in a very large measure for introducing English language teaching in the valley and brought in many innovative practices into the school system. He introduced games and swimming as parts of the character-building programme, which produced some of the best from the valley.

In the mission school, he introduced a system whereby the older boys would learn how to lead and how to teach by giving them an opportunity to become adults for a day. And very rightly he named it the "Free Discipline Day."

Immediately after the bell rang, all the teachers disappeared from the scene and handed over the classes to students of the senior classes who had been selected earlier for this assignment. I and my cousin, were in the sixth class and it fell to our lot to have Hreday as our teacher for the day for that period.

What a contrast it was. It would seem as if Hreday was suddenly transformed from a youngster who played with us into a serious strict adult. To reinforce the image, he carried a scale with him and started lecturing without a preamble. There was a din, but he suddenly shouted and caned a few ringleaders in the front rows and soon a hush and then peace descended on the class and he seriously began teaching us some subject, which I have to my regret forgotten.

The transformation was complete. To my eyes, it seemed as if he had been a teacher for ever and with his eyes darting everywhere looking for mischief mongers, he looked every inch the epitome of perhaps Oliver Goldsmith's village school master or perhaps Mr. Chipps of James Hillton or a combination of both.

Soon the bell rang and the class was over and the teacher left. And some one else came in for the next class. The rest of the day is a blur in my memory, but that day I found out how an opportunity can change a personality.

Hreday is today holder of two Doctorates and a Professor of Neuro Medicine in New Jersey, U.S.A.

"Marm Time" (Morning Time)

In the whole of India, being a tropical country, summer holidays are the longest for the children. But in Kashmir, Himachal, Uttaranchal and the hill districts of West Bengal such as Darjeeling, it is not the summer holidays, which are the longest, but the winter holidays. In the Kashmir valley, the winter vacation would begin in late November or early December and end in mid February.

Many years ago, the people in the valley felt that the summer heat was intolerable of course, by valley standards.

What the Kashmiris called hot was cool and pleasant in the rest of India. Somehow, the authorities decided that children should not be made to go to school during the hot summer days. Therefore, they introduced what was called Morning time.

Of course, the children called it Marm time and so did the housewives. It was a welcome change for the children to have to get up early and go to school at 7 a.m. whereas they were used to going school normally at 10.00 a.m. But for them it was fun and there were other advantages. The school would close at 12.00 and they had plenty of time to play.

It is not quite clear whether the morning school timings were introduced in all schools in the valley, but I distinctly remember that they were indeed enforced in the Mission school at Fatehkadal.

As communication and information expanded, children gradually started becoming bold compared to their earlier shy and generally obedient nature. Generally most of them would listen as the teacher droned on whatever he was teaching. Questions were hardly asked, doubts were mostly unheard of and school was do as the teacher says. But there were certain boys who were exceptions to the rule. For instance, there was this bold young fellow from an affluent family who was caught by the teacher for not paying attention.

When asked what he was doing he replied that he was looking out of the window. The teacher out of sheer curiosity made the mistake of asking him as to what he saw that was very interesting. His reply has gone into the annals, but here it is for what it is worth. "Sir I just saw a beautiful woman, I was hoping I would get a wife like her" In Kashmiri, the nuances are far sharper.

Puraat hish zanane geshim
Would love to have such a robust, plump woman.

The Astrologer was right

One upon a time, there lived a man who after 18 years of service decided to take one-year furlough. As he was leaving for his one-year vacation, he was stopped a little distance away from the place from where he had started. He was told that he had been recalled to duty. His leave was cancelled.

He worked in a far off place for years and then suddenly the Government decided that the post he held had become redundant. The post was abolished and our man was without a job but he had his right over his original job and it was expected that he would go back to it. Meanwhile, his daughter was getting married. He celebrated his daughter's marriage and was going to take a decision on his future.

On a sunny day, he started walking towards the office where he had worked earlier having now decided that he would go back to his original job. As he was passing through a locality (Zaindar Mohalla) where his family astrologer lived, he decided to pay him a visit. In traditional Hindu families in Kashmir, the family priest is also the astrologer and he casts the horoscopes of all those born in the families whom he serves. Normally, all horoscopes cast by him had duplicates, one copy for the person concerned and one for record kept by the astrologer in his own house.

After the initial greeting, our man asked the astrologer to have a look at his horoscope. The astrologer took a few minutes to glance through it and said:

Everything is fine for the time being, there will be no change

But that is impossible. I have been relieved of my job. So, where is the question of my going back to the same job in the same place. There must be some mistake Jyotshiji.

There is no mistake, you are going back to the same place to the same table to the same office. May be, you will be given the job of lifting stones like a coolie, but in terms of respect, prestige and salary you will be facing no change. You will be respected again as you were earlier. That is my final prediction. Please tell me when it happens.

There was no arguing with such a flat, determined, assertion. The man nodded paid him a little money and left his house. He started walking on the main road and a few minutes later a car came fast from the opposite direction, almost passed him and suddenly screeched to a halt. The driver backed until it came abreast with the man.

Out stepped a senior civil servant who told him that the Chief Minister wanted to see him very urgently. He was bundled into the car and taken to the CM's Office.

We have taken a decision to open a new trade organization and we have already set up showrooms in major cities and your city from where you have recently come is on the list. I want you to go forthwith back to Amritsar where you will use not only your former staff members but also the premises of your earlier office. I want you to leave tomorrow. There will be no change in your salary and entitlements. It will be as though you never left your previous job in the same place.

Our man was dazed. What the astrologer had said an hour back had come so accurately true that it was frightening. Needless to say, our man went and shocked his previous office staff who had just two weeks earlier given him a farewell party, by occupying the same seat that he had vacated two weeks earlier.

Island in the Sun

How accurate is astrology? Many have asked this question but few have answered it satisfactorily. Let us give you another instance.

There was this young man in his thirties working in an organisation. Ambitious yes, but he did not find an opportunity to fulfil his desire to go abroad. One fine day, he decided to apply for a scholarship or fellowship in America. Nothing happened, not even a rejection slip, then he gradually gave up dreaming of going up abroad and concentrated on improving his position in the company he worked.

Three years passed and one fine day a senior colleague persuaded him to come with him to a friend of his who was an astrologer. After the initial greetings, he asked for his particulars.

What particulars

Your name, date and time of birth, place of birth

He obliged and the astrologer asked him to come the following week on Sunday to hear about his future.

By April 14, 1979, you will not be in India. You will live abroad for almost a year "But where will I go, can't you tell me." "I can't tell you the place but I can tell you what it will be like. You will be in a place which will be surrounded by water on all sides."

"Perhaps I will be marooned like Robinson Crusoe on an island," our young man said trying to be funny.

Of course, he thought it was a ploy by the astrologer to extract some money from him. Then he looked at the calendar it was December 1978. He thought to himself that it was only a few months away. He could check out the prediction. In any case, he did not believe what the astrologer said. He paid the customary fee and went away.

Several months passed, he forgot all about it. Then one fine day in February 1979 he received a letter from America selecting him for a fellowship in communication studies. At first, he couldn't believe it, and then he looked at the place from where the letter had come. It was the Honolulu Island in the Hawaiian Archipelago, so the second part of the prediction also seemed to have come true.

Once he was over the shock, he set about making preparations for going to America. His prepaid Air ticket arrived, but while he looked at the route and the places, he didn't notice the dates.

Came the great day when he flew from Bangalore to Madras, Singapore, Hong Kong, Tokyo and finally landed at Honolulu International Airport in the United States. He was a little dazed as he collected his luggage and suddenly his eye fell on the calendar hanging on the wall.

It was April 14, 1979 correct to the day, the date that the astrologer had predicted.

The Sound Of Music

Grandfather Baghwan Das Sapru's brother had four sons. Out of these four, he gave away one son in adoption to his relatives who lived close by practically next to Razdan Kocha.

His name was Niranjan Nath Trisal and he used to stay at his adopted parents' house and would frequently come to the Sapru house and also stay there. From the beginning, he had an ear for music but given our economic state (both in the adopted family and his original family) he could not be sent to a music school. Normal schooling was started which after some time petered out. The most remarkable thing that one can remember about this diamond of a man was that he learnt his music from the most primitive instruments. And thereby hangs a tale.

On the ground floor in most of the houses at ground level inside the rooms was such that a man could sit on the floor next to the window and watch the scene outside. The wooden plank out of which the lower portion of the window was made was thin and if you thumped it with your hand it would produce a sound and become a kind of primitive substitute tabla, especially if you used both your hands, one on the outside and the other on the inside.In Kashmiri, this part of the window is called "Damdhar."

This was his first musical instrument. But whenever he thumped the dhamdhar, he would incur the displeasure of all the elders and often get chased out of the house. Most growing boys especially adolescents always explore the kitchen so that they can find something to eat at odd times. Once, Niranjan or Nera as his contemporaries called him, sauntered into the kitchen, suddenly his eyes lit up with pleasure. What he saw was a strainer made of thin leather, which would produce a lovely musical sound in his expert hands.

Poor man, he had to go through all kinds of hell to get himself a job and that too, job that his family and the community and the relatives considered respectable. It is very strange, looking back that while teaching as a profession was lauded, that of a drawing master and a band master were looked down upon. And so poor Nera Trisal had to struggle outside the home, learn the job of playing all the instruments in the orchestra and conducting it as a team and eventually he landed a job as a band master in a school and that gave him a regular income, made him respectable enough. He got married and raised a family.

The best part of his life to my mind and that of hundreds of his admirers was the public adulation that he received and revelled in. By the time, our generation was growing up, he was in his prime and the memorable occasions were when he could show his prowess during a parade and would lead the band that would lead the school team in a procession through the main streets of Srinagar especially the main road from which leads the lane to his house.

In 1951, Pandit Nehru came to Srinagar and there was a procession of schoolboys and other contingents, which went through the main road. It was a lovely summer afternoon, with a pleasant breeze and thousand of people looking out of the windows of the houses, which lined two the sides of the road. And of course, our hero Niranjan Nath was leading with that long magical stick which he kept throwing into the air and catching it without faltering in keeping up with the tempo and speed of movement.

I was in one of the houses glued to the window watching the parade and looking out for him because I suddenly discovered that his wife, children, relatives both from the Trisal and Sapru families had gathered to watch him march past. As the procession reached Razdan Kocha, everyone suddenly pointed towards his impressive figure resplendent in uniform with the tora of his turban flying majestically in the air and right at that spot he simple looked up smiling probably for the benefit of his wife who was watching from the window. To make it a memorable occasion, he held the stick and threw it up, caught it expertly and having done that, without batting an eye marched on smartly.

He used to come quite regularly to see my father. And on various occasions I noticed and heard that he had a lifelong fascination for the humble potato. Among the Kashmiris, there is a dish known as "Dum Aloo" which is potato cooked in chilli based red masala with thick gravy, normally an essential ingredient on special guest dinners or weddings. Today, anywhere in India or even abroad, the Dum Aloo is a five star hotel dish which can only be ordered and consumed by the rich and the famous.

But my favourite Niranajan Nath of the band master fame loved it and would eat it as often as possible. He was a versatile man. You don't find many like him anymore.

10

Eviction Unabated

EVEN before the 1989-90 attacks on Pandits in the Kashmiri Valley by the Pakistan inspired insurgency, there was a steady eviction of Pandits from the Valley. The instrument of eviction was very simple. No scope for jobs and shrinking opportunities for higher technical education.

Mr. M. Rasgotra, former Foreign Secretary of Government of India has summed it up with necessary details.

> At the turn of the century, the population of the Kashmir Valley's Pandits was close to a million. Today, no more than a few thousand remain. More than 300,000, driven out by Muslim fanatics at gunpoint in 1990-91, are living precariously in refugee camps in Jammu, Delhi and elsewhere.
>
> Cleansing the valley of its Pandits has been going on since July 1931, when the first Muslim-Hindu riot took place there. Even under the Dogra rule, the Kashmiri Pandits were not favoured in the matter of recruitment to government service. Feeling vulnerable and neglected following the riot, they started moving out to Indian cities. A few adventurous ones left for foreign lands. Some 30,000 to 40,000 families are said to have moved out of Kashmir in the 1931-41 decade.
>
> According to the 1941 census, the Kashmir valley's population comprised 15 per cent Pandits as against 83 per cent Muslims. 25 or even 30 per cent would be a more realistic figure of the Pandits at that time. Kashmir's censuses, conducted by junior, local Muslim officials are notorious

for describing Pandit households as Muslim families. The 1941 census marks the beginnig of a statistical assault on the Pandit's numbers.

India's independence and Kashmir's accession did little to improve the fortunes of the valley's Pandits numbering about 800,000 at that time. They remained as vulnerable as before. Virtually none of the billions in so-called development funds poured into the state by the Union Government reached them. For that matter, nor did much of that bounty reach the backward Muslim communities, such as Gujjars and Bakarwals.

At the time of Pakistan's invasion of Kashmir in 1947, some Pandit families did flee to safety in India, but most of them returned to their homes after the raiders were expelled. In a curious development, the state administration floated figures varying from 80,000 to 120,000 as representing the number of the Pandits remaining in the valley. After visiting Kashmir, Ram Manohar Lohia mentioned in a letter to Nehru that no more than 80,000 Pandits were left in the valley.

The effect of all this was to deny the Pandits their due representation in the State legislature. The design was further advanced by gerrymandering the constituencies in the Pandit-dominated areas of Srinagar, Anantnag, etc., to eliminate any possibility of the community putting up and electing candidates of its choice. To create an illusion of fairness in the matter, the administration did, however, ensure that one but never more than one Pandit found his way to the State Legislature, often with Muslim voters support. This also helped to justify to some extent the statistical violence on the Pandits numbers.

The 1981 census put the Pandits number at a little over 124,000 in a total population of 3.1 million. Their share in the valley's population was down to five per cent as against 15 per cent in the 1941 census with a corresponding rise in the percentage of Muslims, up from 83 per cent in 1941 to 95 per cent in 1981. The enormity of this injustice perpetrated by supposedly secular and democratic Government on this hapless community stood exposed in 1990, when 300,000 Pandits — men, women kand children — fled the valley under threat of the terrorist's guns and poured into hastily — organised refugee camps in Jammu and other places.

The statistical assault continued, this exposure notwithstanding. The 1991 census places the Pandits share of the Valley's population at 0.1 per cent which would translate into a head count of 3,000. I believe some 50,000 or more are still in the valley and another unaccounted 100,000 or so temporarily sheltered with relatives in Jammu and elsewhere in India.

Our own human rights enthusiasts, ever ready to smear the image of our armed forces engaged in fighting Pakistan's dirty proxy war in Kashmir, have done little to highlight the Pandits plight. Worse still, our media's casual, almost cynical, treatment of this slow — motion tragedy, thoughtless and repeated description of these victims of denial, deprivation and terror as "migrants," has inured the country to this grievous wrong. It has dulled the nation's sense of responsibility towards an abused and aggrieved minority and lulled the authorities into complacency and inaction.

In all the current fuss in New Delhi concerning economic and political packages for Kashmir and plans to conduct elections to normalize the situation there, no one seems to spare a thought for the Pandits. The modalities of their participation in the elections, and the question of their rehabilitation in Kashmir, ought to figure in these packages and electoral plans.

— Aug. 26, 1995, *Indian Express.*

Vanishing Species

From the early 30s to late 80s is a period of nearly half century. One journalist who can be described as one of the father figures of jounalism in Kashmir was Pandit R.K. Kak. He reported Kashmir in the National dailies in depth. Highly respected, he was perhaps the most knowledgeable person who was familiar with every aspect of Kashmir.

This writer had the good fortune of knowing this extraordinary journalist during his last visit to the Kashmir Valley. One day, we had a discussion in 1987 in his Pratap Park house. He told me the following.

After the Pakistani invasion had been halted and the raiders pushed back, normal administration was restored. In the early 50s one of the senior secretaries of the GOI visited Kashmir and R.K. Kak went to meet him. During the meeting Kak, asked about the fate of the minority in the Valley. He meant Kashmiri Pandits of course.

The worthy member of the steel frame categorically declared that the GOI did not care what happened to the minority and they (GOI) would not hesitate to sacrifice this miniscule minority if its interests dictated so. Kak was horrified to hear this and related this to me nearly 37 years later. A prophetic declaration it was, but the sequel is given in the words of author Anil Maheshwari in his book "*Crescent Over Kashmir.*"

Bansi Parimu, the internationally known painter says:

> Parimu asked S.B. Chavan the then Union Minister for Human Resources — who had visited Srinagar in 1986 in connection with a project for the wildlife conservation in the Valley, "I believe you are interested in the preservation of the endangered species of stags." Answering in the affirmative, Chavan said, "It is a project much after the heart of Governor Jagmohan and I too am interested." Parimu asked, "But why cannot you do something about the other endangered species here?" "Which endangered species?" asked Chavan. Pat came the Even Parimu who was hounded out by terrorists from the Valley and died in wilderness in New Delhi in 1991, did not know that he was making a prophesy about the fate of the minuscule minority in the Valley.
>
> — From Anil Maheshwari in "*Crescent Over Kashmir.*"

> The eminent journalist and writer Arun Shourie, while complimenting the Kashmiri Hindus on their efforts, confessed during the World Conference of Kashmiri Pandits in Geneva: "You have done far better than we Punjabis in responding to the challenges posed by terrorism and fundamentalism. The outbursts of Dr. Gh. Nabi Fai, the leader of Kashmir American council in front of Pandit delegates in Geneva, after Pakistan was forced to withdraw the crucial resolution against India in NHRC, was only a compliment to Pandits. "We were defeated by Kashmiri Pandits and not by the Government of India, he said."
>
> — Dr. Ajay Chrungoo, *Vitasta*

Persecution and Forced Exodus
Says the Spirit of Kashmiri Pandits Personified:

I fled along with thousands of others, on foot, and on horse backs through dense and dark forests, crossing 9000 to 14000 feet high peaks of Pir Panjal. *En route* to the plains, many died of hunger, most of them detoured to Bhaderwah and Kishtwar from Batawath (Pandit Route) which has got metamorphosed into Batote. Some settled there, while some dragged on and found refuge in Allahabad, Varanasi, Delhi (at Sitaram Bazar), Lucknow (in Kashmiri Mohalla) and even as far as in Assam to save themselves from the barbarians and the vandals.

The condition was no different between 1320 and 1948 onwards. On a Navreh (New Year) function held at the Constitution Club (Now called Vithal Bhai Patel House) in the year 1950, Late K.N. Katju, the them Home Minister of India, said, "Then we fled on foot or on horse backs and now we use vehicular transport, conditions have not changed." Late Jawahar Lal Nehru, Late Smt. Rameshori and Late Dr. Sidh Nath Kaul, all were present.

— K.L. Moza, *Vitasta*, 1999-2000, Noida

11

Tomorrow is Forever

From Pen To Theodolite and Byte

THE professional profile of a community, especially as small as the half a million Kashmiri Pandits community, can tell a lot about the value system and professional preference of the community. Because of the physical limitations of the venturing beyond the mountain borders of the valley and the peace that prevailed in the valley from 1846 to 1947, no one was interested in leaving the valley, even for a short while to professionally qualify himself.

For five generations (in historic terms one century produces five generations each comprising and spanning twenty years), simultaneously, with the setting up of the Dogra rule and improvement in transport and communications, Kashmiri Pandits began to take interest in the rest of the world, which initially was India and more than that the province of Punjab being the closest by virtue of the Jhelum Valley road, which took the traveller from J&K to Rawalpandi in British India.

Until 1947, there were very few Pandits who were either doctors or engineers or even higher education teachers like lecturers and professors. Although the word "Karkun" means a person who has a skill, it was for purposes of the Pandits, the skill to wield a pen but not a screwdriver or a hammer.

Those few, who did go out to qualify themselves through higher education, invariably went to Lahore or Lucknow or Allahabad or Aligarh. Most of them studied humanities and the few who could be counted on a finger tips also studied medicine or engineering in the northern India.

Out of these few, even a fewer number went aboard mostly to U.K for furthering their expertise. In this, the doctors took the lead. While in north India outside Kashmir, many of them came into contact with those Pandits who had been victims of persecution in the valley during Aurangzeb's time and the Afghan rule and migrated to British India, and other princely states in north India.

It must be conceded that considering their small number compared to those in the valley, they did exceedingly well in the services, although here too the Karkun mentality prevailed. Most of the plains Kashmiri Pandits joined either the ICS if they could or the provincial services or the various departments of the judicial profession. Even in civil service the preferred general administration, revenue, judicial and education.

Meanwhile, in the valley, the doctors who returned, got good appointments and gradually they became objects of admiration and emulation within the community. Thus the horizons of the young men widened and they began to move away from the B.A and M.A mentality. The catalyst for this was the availability, then, of science courses in the S.P. and Amar Singh colleges. In fact, according to N.N. Moza, for the first time in 1938 eight Pandits boys graduated with the B. Sc. degree.

Thus a slow kind of dispersal of interest with a widening choice of profession began and as the freedom movement neared independence, the community realized that under popular rule, Pandits would not get any more jobs as they were getting earlier. Besides this, the number of Muslims by 1947, going in for English education had increased and subconsciously, Pandits began to search for fresh avenues outside Kashmir to qualify themselves professionally.

Leaving aside the Pakistani aggression of 1947, Kashmir also went through a tremendous expansion of economic activity after independence and the watershed was the first Five Year Plan. Funds were allotted by the Central Government and schemes were formulated. These in Kashmir mainly centred round roads, buildings, canals, bridges, etc., in short there was a huge demand for civil engineers.

At this point of time in the early fifties, a majority of Pandits boys, who would earlier have completed B.A or B.Sc, left at the F.Sc stage and applied for civil engineering courses being offered in various colleges in the country for which the Government of India had reserved certain number of seats for candidates from Kashmir. Since all of them could not get admission to degree courses (B.E), most of the unsuccessful ones went in for two or three year diploma courses.

As there were not enough Muslim candidates in the fifties, most of the posts were filled for the first time by technical graduates and diploma holders from the Kashmiri Pandit community. In fact, there was a rash of such people who were appointed as overseers. This was a post created before 1947 in British India, copied by the princely states and continued in Kashmir even after independence. Today, its equivalent is the Junior Engineer.

This had a cascading affect on social and matrimonial values within the community. Overseers suddenly became favourites, of matchmakers and parents of eligible girls, as prospective sons-in-law. Thus the old preference for F.A and B.A disappeared and the clerk was replaced by the Overseer — the pen by the theodolite.

In the sixties and seventies, gradually the number of qualified Muslim candidates increased considerably and quite a number of Pandit boys who went out of the Valley to qualify themselves, took up jobs outside Kashmir. Gradually this became a practice. The son leaving for higher education and taking up a job and the parents staying back with the father by then having retired from service. The very first batch of overseers retired in the early eighties and wherever a Pandit retired, the job went to a Kashmiri Muslim candidate.

Thus the exodus was economic driven. It started in 1947 and by the middle eighties, hardly any jobs were available. The Pandits had effectively been thrown out except for the last link — parents and grandparents who lived there, the house and those who still had a few more years of service left before retirement in the state. The 1989-90 killings and terrorism was the final push in the plan which in the twentieth century began with the 1931 riots inspired and aided by the Punjab Muslim League and abetted by British, Political Department of the Viceroy of India.

Thus in a short span of thirty years, Pandits have moved from being clerks or Karkuns to all aspects of technology, medicine, engineering, electronics and any other field which seems attractive to young men and women. In the fore going, no mention has been made about girls. From the late 40s, there was a tremendous pressure and demand to educate our girls and today one can be proud that they are in practically every field in which boys have done well. Overall, the community has cent percent literacy rate.

The earlier glitter or attraction for Government jobs has totally disappeared since guaranteed jobs are no longer in fashion especially with the "Mai Baap Sarkar". Even the community's share of IAS and IPS has gone down. Today, it is trade industries and commerce both in India and abroad.The Private sector today is where the action is.

But all said and done, the fascination of the Kashmiri Pandits with the pen today (read computer also) is still there. That is why, we find a large number of them working as journalists, writers, artistes, musicians, singers, painters, film actors, authors, theatre personalities and social workers.

Bibliography

Bamzai, P.N.K., *Cultural & Political History of Kashmir* (Vols. 1-3).

Bakshi, S.R., *Kashmir Valley & its Culture,* Kashmir: History & People.

Bazaz, P.N., *Daughters of the Vitasta.*

Bhatt, S., *Kashmiri Pandits: A Cultural Heritage.*

Kaul, R.K., *Names & Nicknames of Kashmir.*

Kaul, Mohan Lal, *Kashmir, Wail of a Valley, Atrocity & Terror.*

Kalla, K. Aloke, *Kashmiri Pandits & Their Diversity.*

Kaul, Anand Pandit, *The Kashmiri Pandit.*

Maheswari, Anil, *Crescent over Kashmir.*

Madan, T.N., *A Study of Pandits of Rural Kashmir.*

Pant, Kusum, *The Kashmiri Pandit, Story of a Community in Exile.*

Sapru, S., *Lost Shrangri La — Glimpses of Ancient Kashmir.*

Sender, Henny, *The Kashmiri Pandits.*

Tyndale Biscoe, C.E., *Men in the Making, Kashmir in Light & Shade.*

———, *Tyndale Biscoe of Kashmir* (autobiography).

———, *Coaching in Kashmir.*

———, *Coxing in Kashmir.*

———, *Paddling in Kashmir.*

———, *Towung in Kashmir.*

———, *Kashmir & its inhabitants.*

———, *Travels in Kashmir, Ladakh & Iskardo.*

Wali, I.K., & Wali, M.K., *Kashmir Pandits — A Social Survey.*